The Brick

Zig,

Keep the music going!

Best always,

Lee Witt

2010

The Brick House Band

How an Ordinary Mid-Life Couple Created a Business Phenomenon

Lee Witt

Outskirts Press, Inc.
Denver, Colorado

The BrickHouse Band
How an Ordinary Mid-Life Couple Created a Business Phenomenon

v2.0

Outskirts Press, Inc.
http://www.outskirtspress.com

ISBN: 978-1-4327-4986-6

Library of Congress Control Number: 2009940770

PRINTED IN THE UNITED STATES OF AMERICA

This book is dedicated to all those who said we couldn't.
You gave me the resolve to ensure that we could.

And to Brooke,
Who always *knew* we could.

Contents

Preface

There have been several thousand books on personal growth, business and leadership written over the last few decades. They all claim to be unique. Some claim to have "the secret" to wealth and abundance. Others claim that productivity and happiness are as easy as 1-2-3. Still others have the "key" to business success. After all of this, why on earth would we need another book?

Because chances are, you've never read one written by and about people who are JUST LIKE YOU!

We are not Army Rangers, Navy SEALs, or Air Force pilots. Those individuals are made from the sturdiest of humanity's potential. They are true American heroes. They are the best of the best and we love them.

But we are not them.

We are not licensed psychotherapists, Wall Street analysts, or charming physicians like Dr. Oz, although we respect their work and contributions.

But we are not them.

We are not business tycoons like Donald Trump or media moguls like Oprah Winfrey.

We are definitely not them.

Most likely, we are just like you.

We are dental hygienists, law clerks, certified public accountants, waitresses, business consultants and aerospace employees.

We are just like you... and boy have we got a story to tell.

To our knowledge, no one has ever written a personal growth book with leadership lessons that apply to all businesses – while having an artistic product as its base.

That's right; we're a band – a cover band at that. But we've been on an amazing journey. And now we've reached a destination. We began as an impractical idea and now we're *the best damn cover band in the western United States of America!*

Why should you care? Because to succeed at any level, whether as an individual, a businessperson, an athlete or an artist, you need a particular toolkit for that specific skill set or application. This book will cross all of those boundaries to give you that toolkit. You will be given a performance methodology that if practiced, will take you from the bottom to the top. You will gain access to the personal qualities, business applications, and artistic sensibilities that will enable you to take any idea – and make it a reality.

Even more importantly, we'll show you how to do it when all odds are against you.

Why? Because chances are...

We're just like you.

Introduction

We were sitting in the Seattle area's largest casino. Brooke and I had been married for one year - just an average American, middle-aged couple out on a date. We were watching a popular local cover band perform on a gigantic stage. They were playing our favorite dance music. A giant-sized movie screen projected the band's image to those in the back. The dance floor was filled with hundreds of joyous people. The energy was electric.

As I watched, I began to reflect. I wondered how I would measure up if I was up there performing on that stage. I wondered the same about my wife. I thought about what kinds of musical capabilities we both had. By day, Brooke was a certified public accountant. At one time, she had been a competitive ballroom dancer. She had also hosted karaoke at a small restaurant on Friday nights for ten consecutive years. Obviously, that qualified her as a music lover. While she didn't see herself as an extraordinary singer, she had a four-octave vocal range. She also had extraordinary stage presence.

I had just finished my fifteenth year in the aerospace

business. My musical background was best described as "a great deal of musical talent – squandered." I had been labeled a child prodigy on piano. In my teens and early twenties, I played piano bars to help put myself through college. But eventually I burned out. I couldn't picture myself playing smoke-filled Holiday Inn lounges for the rest of my life. As a result, I began to focus on my aerospace career, sports and other interests. I had always had a tremendous amount of self-discipline, but never in music. Unlike everything else, music came easily for me. And although I listened to a lot of music, after I turned 25, I rarely thought about performing.

As I got older, that began to change. It was as if something inside of me was trying to get out. Certain artistic sensibilities were being rekindled. I once again felt the urge to play. At the age of 43, I purchased a small digital piano. Just like riding a bike, it all began to come back. Then at the age of 45, I met Brooke. Her love for music was infectious. Shortly after we married, she began singing backup vocals for a local cover band. Soon, I was sitting in on keyboards and enjoying it immensely. Having mostly been a solo act in my formative years, it was great fun being part of a team. Having also had an extensive athletic and business background, *I could see the parallels between winning sports teams, profitable businesses and successful bands. There were certain characteristics common to each.*

On that particular night in the casino, Brooke and I had the same thought at exactly the same time. We looked at one another. We knew exactly what the other was thinking. We wanted to perform on that stage. In fact, we had a burning desire to be up there. We wanted to bring the same kind of energy and joy to those people on the dance floor that they were experiencing that very moment. We wanted to provide that same feeling – and we wanted to feel it ourselves. But we knew there was only one way to make that happen.

We would have to form our own band.

CHAPTER 1

Making Something from Nothing: Maybe Anything *IS* Possible!

BrickHouse Principle Number 1: You must understand where you're going and why.

Everyone said we were too old. They said we were too inexperienced. We hardly knew any musicians. We didn't have an agent. And if that wasn't enough, the market place for live music was glutted. There were well over eight hundred bands in the Seattle area vying for about 50 jobs on any given weekend. And of course, we were too busy parenting and pursuing our careers to put together a band, let alone a successful one. Why, any sane person could figure out that it would take years to put together a band that could play the top venues in the northwest.

Those were the arguments we heard. The consensus among everyone was, "Are you out of your minds?"

In truth, that was a fair question. As it turns out, we were indeed out of our minds, but more on that and how that can be a good thing in chapter three. We understood that the odds were against us. But for most of our lives, Brooke and I had been successful in almost everything we tried. Our experience of multiple successes had given us a certain hubris that made it seem like anything was possible. At some level, we believed that we could create "something from nothing." This book is designed to show you how we did just that – and how you can do it too.

It didn't hurt that we were both extremely competitive. Right or wrong, we loved to compete and we loved to win. If someone told either one of us that we couldn't do something, well, that's all we needed to hear. *We'd show them!*

We thrived on competition. Case in point, we honeymooned on the beautiful tropical island of Curacao. We stayed at one of those all-inclusive island paradise resorts. Unfortunately, the stress of my work combined with the wedding and travel had been too much for my immune system. On the third day of our trip, Brooke took me to the island's doctor. I was feeling quite ill but I was also determined not to spoil our honeymoon vacation. Slightly feverish and pumped full of antibiotics, we finished dinner that evening. I excused myself to go back to our room to wash the sweat off my face. The temperature was in the 90's and I just needed a moment to pull myself together. I didn't want Brooke to see how badly I felt. My voice was completely gone. My energy was sapped. As I headed back to the room, I heard someone on the microphone at our ocean-side dining facility say something about a big dance contest coming up.

Relieved that I didn't have to be a part of any dance contest, I went back to the room for a few minutes. When

I returned, I saw Brooke standing on the stage motioning me to come up. I heard myself croak, "No, this can't be happening."

Brooke had entered us in the dance contest. God help me. The marriage was less than a week old and I was ready to end it. She, of course, was a phenomenal dancer, having won several New York Hustle competitions and heaven knows what else. I had taken some salsa lessons while we were dating. While certainly not rhythmically-challenged, I was hardly a competitive dancer.

As it turned out, this was billed as a Latin dance contest. Out of nine couples, we were the only English speaking couple in the contest. There would be eight different dances performed. I was comforted to find that even though a Latin dance contest, they had included R&B and rock along with salsa, merengue, tango and others. As we began, I felt dizzy with fever. But I also felt my competitive juices kick in. I could see that Brooke's had as well. She was going for it. But I still needed to be certain as to just how seriously she was taking this. During the first dance I whispered in her ear, "You want to win, don't you."

Under her breath she responded, "Yes."

It was on.

I figured my best strategy was a lot of hips and understated masculine movement while styling towards Brooke. She literally took over the dance floor. I would sort of stand there in a matador's posture while she spun herself out in some ridiculously amazing move. Then she would spin back to me and the crowd would ooh and aah.

This reminded me of the time when, as a twelve-year old, I had my one experience as a hockey player. Basketball was my chosen winter sport but on this day, it was hockey. A bunch of my friends and I went outdoors to a frozen lake. I owned ice skates but had never used them. Because I didn't know how to skate, everyone said I should be the goalie. My job would be to block the opponent's shots as they tried to shoot the puck into the net. This would require almost no skating. Using my trusty first baseman's mitt and a stick that was larger than me, I spent three of the most pain-ridden hours of my life. Every time someone would shoot at the goal, I would try and get out of the way. After all, the puck was hard, frozen and it hurt when it hit you. Being of sound mind, I wanted to avoid pain at all costs.

But inevitably, in trying to get out of the way, I would fall down. After all, I couldn't skate. The puck would slam off of my body and everyone would yell, "Great save!" In spite of myself, I was accidentally doing a great job. That's exactly how I felt dancing with Brooke. I was accidentally doing a great job – simply trying to get out of the way! If I couldn't exactly help, at least I could try not to hurt. It reminded me of one of the great tenants of the Hippocratic Oath that has served physicians for years, "Above all, do no harm."

As we continued, I tried to watch the other dancers out of the corner of my eye. It became apparent that Brooke was the best dancer on the floor. All I had to do was look confident, carry a great posture and mostly, do no harm. Remembering the Hippocratic Oath, I thought to myself, *don't screw this up*. I felt like the magician's assistant who poses and styles adoringly towards the magician after he releases the doves from his shirtsleeves.

The idea of *doing no harm* may not seem like an impressively aggressive mindset. However, in business, great numbers of people too often dash off in a direction that ties up company assets, wastes people's time and delivers nothing to the company's bottom line. It begins when they think they have a great idea. Then they remember that someone once told them, "It's better to ask forgiveness than permission." So they picture themselves as Mr. or Ms. Business Maverick and begin wreaking havoc all over their environment. In reality, unless they've been chartered by their boss to go off and implement this great idea, they'd be far better off starting their own company and sponsoring it themselves. Otherwise, they end up creating more work and causing problems for everyone. In many cases, it would have been better had they done nothing.

There are many other ways that harm can be done. Sometimes company executives will send different people out to do the same job. They do this just to hedge their bets in the hope that the job gets done. They figure that at least one out of the five people they send off will accomplish the task. But they're wasting valuable human resources. Or they'll create work as a strategy to keep people occupied in an effort to disguise their own ignorance or lack of competence. If you're a leader, don't do this. Stop doing harm. As in my dancing with Brooke, sometimes doing less actually contributes more. After all, you want to be remembered for the problems you solved, not the ones you created.

The dance contest went on. At approximately three to four minutes per dance, we danced about 30 consecutive minutes. We were soaked in sweat, absolutely drenched. I was completely spent and greatly relieved when it was over. Although I still felt feverish and was now dizzy, I had made it. From what I could tell, I actually thought we might have won.

The judges conferred. Horrified, I heard them say in three different languages so that everyone at the venue could understand, "We have a tie. We will have a dance-off between three couples. The winner will be decided by applause."

I bent over putting my hands on my knees. Not a winner's body language. As stricken as I must have looked, Brooke looked a bit shell-shocked as well. It had probably been a few years since she had danced competitively. The 90-plus heat was taking its toll on the entrants from the USA. And there were no *"USA…USA!"* chants coming from the crowd.

I looked all around for a water bottle. A young woman with a group from Venezuela saw my distress and brought me a drink. Then I looked at Brooke and said in a frog-like croak, "Let's just win this, okay?" Too exhausted to speak, she nodded.

Practically delirious with fever, I danced the overtime. I remember nothing about it. Brooke must have gathered herself and pushed through her fatigue. From what people told me afterwards, she had just too much polish, glamour and charisma to be beaten. Or it could have been that they took pity on the middle-aged white guy who looked to be at death's door. But at the conclusion of the overtime, we were voted the winning couple by applause. This was my first real introduction to Brooke's competitive fire. It would serve us well down the road.

And I had to admit, I liked it.

The BrickHouse Philosophy says, "Compete until you win"

You can call it the desire to achieve. You can call it the urge to excel. The BrickHouse philosophy calls it the desire to "compete." A lot of people don't like the idea of competing. They feel that if someone wins, then someone else has to lose. And if someone else loses, that's a bad thing.

I understand that train of thought. It's just that I have a slightly different slant on it.

I believe that we live in an abundant universe. I believe that there are enough resources for everyone to win. I routinely give my resources away because they don't define me and there's plenty more where that came from. But at the most fundamental level, the only way I can gather wealth and resources is by producing a product or service that someone will pay for. This sometimes means I have to produce it *better* or *cheaper* than someone else. If I succeed in doing that, it could possibly be interpreted as *I win*. If I don't produce it better or cheaper it could mean that *I lose*.

I'm fine with that. If I lose, it's up to me to improve my product or service until I win. If I can't, then it is also up to me to find a different product or service to produce. By competing to win, it doesn't mean I have to angrily try and crush my competitors. Not at all. In fact, if we're lucky, maybe there's enough of a market that we can all support ourselves. But I can't control what other people are doing. Therefore, I compete to win. For the BrickHouse Band, winning means that we are the preferred provider of our services for an entire entertainment market. That means bringing what the audience, or customer, wants.

This philosophy stems from a fairly basic business principle: *The customer is always right*. This isn't rocket science and everyone has heard it. So why do so many people, particularly in the arts, seem to miss it entirely? They sometimes act as if they believe the customer is wrong. But the audience, your customer, is never wrong. They simply want what they want. If you want to succeed, you need to provide it. Unless you have a nice endowment from a generous benefactor, it's not about "your art." It's not about what *you* want to do. It's always about the audience and what they're willing to pay for. When they stop paying to see or hear what you do, it's time to get out or adapt. Your customer audience has a right to their preference.

So in a sense, competition is a given. If you are not comfortable with the idea of competing, try this. Simply resolve to be the best you can be without thought of winning or losing. In essence, you're simply competing against yourself. Put your attention on the goal that you're going after. In that way, you're always improving, moving beyond your previous best regardless of what anyone else is doing. Being outstanding generally takes care of everything. In fact, outstanding work is always the best deterrent to discrimination. No one will care how old you are, what color you are, or what gender if they can't live without you. But please understand, if someone else is doing what you're doing, competition exists. Just because you choose not to recognize it won't make it go away.

Fortunately, The BrickHouse Band enjoys competing. We also enjoy winning. But in order to do that, we have to be willing to risk losing. There is no winning without the possibility of loss. And there will be times when you lose. So what. Big deal. A loss is just a loss, nothing more, nothing less. It's not a "dramatic setback" or "tragedy" unless you label it as such.

Furthermore, a loss is only permanent if you give up. The sky is not falling so there is no need for drama. Time spent waving your arms in hysteria just keeps you from looking for a solution that could lead to a win. Losing only means that you may need to shift your strategy or change your approach. Once you've done that, take a breath, smile, get up and start competing again. The BrickHouse philosophy is very simple: You have to want what you're going after very badly. Then you must compete until you win. Winning cures everything.

Yes, it really is that simple.

The BrickHouse Philosophy says, "Always Advance"

"How can it be that simple?" you ask.

Maybe you've suffered what you've called a devastating loss. A death in the family. An illness. Or perhaps you have lost a ton in the stock market. So how does one get up and begin to win again after such a loss?

The BrickHouse philosophy advocates an *Always Advance* attitude. The *Always Advance* attitude is so central to the BrickHouse way of thinking that it has become an entire performance methodology that we'll be revealing throughout this material. It is designed to drive you forward through any and all obstacles until you reach your destination. As such, it will be highlighted in italics hereafter.

Why is it important to *Always Advance*? And why would you want to? Why would you want to advance after a death in the family? Or an illness? Or a loss in the stock market?

I'll give you the answer in the form of another question:

What else is there to do?

Seriously, think about it. What else is there to do? You can grieve. Sure. You can feel sorry for yourself. Absolutely, you'd be completely justified. You can lament your tremendous loss. Certainly, who wouldn't?

But at some point, you need to get up and begin to advance. When and how you do that is up to you. (We believe sooner is better. Time is precious.) But sooner or later, you have to take what you're left with and get up. Then you can begin the process of advancing.

Here's an easily understood business example. Employee turnover in a business is usually a bad thing. There is often a loss in terms of time and money. When training a new person, there's a cost to bringing that person up to speed. While we work to discourage turnover in our band, if someone leaves, we see an opportunity. We use the turnover to our advantage. We employ the *Always Advance* attitude by upgrading that position – every time. No exceptions. Losing an employee is always an opportunity to find someone with even greater skill. It's a chance to find someone who is even more team-oriented. *Always Advance* and trade up.

By holding firm to the *Always Advance* attitude, a band or a company can improve with every change of personnel. After all, isn't it up to us who we hire?

Unfortunately, some lessons need to be learned the hard way. We didn't have an *Always Advance* attitude or methodology when we began. And it cost us. There's an unbelievable amount of unemployed musical talent out in the world. Seriously, there are people that are so good it would make you weep. But what really makes you weep is when you hire them to be in your band – and you find the underlying problem as to why they're not working.

The BrickHouse Philosophy says, "If you're not successful in your life, you won't be successful in our band"

This was not self-evident to us when we began. Because there are so many unbelievably talented singers and musicians out there, we were easily seduced. We didn't realize that sometimes this talent comes with a cost. That cost might be a drug problem, a personality problem, an ego problem or simply an inability to hold any kind of job. Whatever the problem is though, I guarantee it will raise its ugly head if you allow that person to become part of your business.

If you are hiring personnel, simply look at their employment and personal histories. People who have successfully set and achieved goals will obviously have a better chance of success with you. This would seem self-evident but it's the simple things that often get overlooked. Have they finished what they have begun? Are they hungry to succeed? Do they want it badly? Of course nowadays, you can also learn a lot from on-line Facebook and MySpace pages. But the rule of thumb is always, "If they are not successful in their lives, they will not be successful in your band." Don't be seduced by a pretty package. Look more deeply. Quality people will always pay out better in the long run. Screen with diligence.

This leads us to our first success principle. BrickHouse Principle Number 1 states: *You must understand where you are going and why.*

You can have a tremendous competitive desire to win. You can have an attitude of always advancing. You can also have the highest caliber of employees. But if you don't know where you're going, you will flounder. You will splash around in a sea of confusion, floating from event to event with no direction. You may look good while you're doing it, but in reality, you're not going anywhere.

It would seem obvious that an organization or business would have a well-defined destination. Yet there are numerous corporations, businesses, and entertainment acts that have no idea where they're going. They have no identity and they're just shooting at things hoping to hit something. It's okay to shoot but *"You have to actually be aiming at something specific!"*

If you don't believe this, just ask any ten of your employed friends, relatives, or acquaintances if they know what their company's mission is. Ask them to define who their customer is. Ask them what their company's profit margin is and what their company's plan for growth is.

Then ask them what their personal mission statement is.

I'm guessing that their response to almost every question will be, "Huh?"

In order to succeed, you must know 1) who you are, 2) who you want to be, 3) what you're going after and 4) what it will look like when you get there. That way you'll know when you arrive.

You can call it your goal. You can call it your objective, your mission or your target. But you must have a clearly defined end result that you're trying to reach. We call it our *destination* because a destination implies a journey – and a journey is always exciting.

The BrickHouse Band has been on an amazing journey since we began. Brooke and I realized that in order to reach our destination, our band would need an identity. As such, we would have to begin "branding" our product. We began by examining our own individual strengths and weaknesses. Not knowing who our musicians would be, we began by simply building around our own personal capabilities. Then we talked about what kind of band we wanted to become. From this, we began building our own vision and mission statements (see Appendix I) that outlined our destination.

Vision and mission statements for businesses have received a fair amount of criticism in the past few years. Much of that criticism has been justified because too often, highly paid consultants come in and take executives through an exercise that results in a vision and mission that look simply like a hodge-podge of buzzwords. This generally leaves company employees laughing hysterically, or minimally, leaves them cynical.

However, well-done vision and mission statements provide direction and a destination for your business. If you don't want to call them a vision and mission, call them something else. All they need to convey is a clear idea of who you will become when you have succeeded. To the extent possible, you should *act as if* you already have. It's truly amazing how the world will step aside and let you pass when you know where you're headed.

Vision and mission statements can be extended beyond your business. Building a personal vision and mission is just as important as doing so for your business. Why is it important to have personal vision and mission statements? It's important because *it allows you to consciously choose your identity*. Why let a personality test, a parent, a teacher, or something a friend told you when you were in the third grade decide what kind of a person you are. Identify your ideal self. Decide how you want to be and what you want to be able to do. If it will serve your purpose to be outgoing, decide that you will take on the characteristics of an outgoing person. You can decide what that looks like. Then act the part. Become that person today. Soon, it will no longer be an act. It's completely up to you who you choose to be. Isn't it? If not you, who then?

As you look at who you want to become, recognize that your business is only as good as the people in it. That will obviously include you. Take the time to think about why you're on earth. What are you here to do? Where are you going? Who are you serving? In life, who is your customer? Decisions become a lot easier to make when you know who you are and what you're about. You can choose your personal identity just as you can choose your corporate identity. Most likely, they can serve one another and help you reach your selected destination.

Without a personal vision and mission, you risk spending your life on things that do not matter to you. A life without direction or purpose will leave you feeling weak and discouraged. You will find yourself waiting for things to happen when in fact, you could be making things happen. If you have the courage to live your vision and mission, you might just find yourself living a grand adventure. The BrickHouse experience has taught us that life will reward us at the level we are willing to engage it.

Just as important as where you're going but often overlooked is *why.* Why are you going where you're going? Why are you doing this? What is your motivation for taking on a project? What do you hope to get out of it? What emotional need will it meet? Answers to these questions will help you get to the bottom of your *why*.

Most books on business and personal growth don't spend enough time on *why*. The great 19th century German poet, philosopher and critic, Friedrich Nietzsche said, "He who has a why can bear with any how." His point? If why you are doing something is important enough, you can put up with almost anything to get it done. That is why it is absolutely essential to know why you're doing what you're doing.

Are you doing it for money? Are you doing it for love? Are you doing it to serve the planet? Are you doing it for recognition? Are you doing it as a fun hobby? Are you doing it to become closer to your spouse or children? Are you doing it to be healthier?

Only you can answer *why*. In order to be successful, you must answer it and your reasons must be compelling enough to keep you motivated through the inevitable challenges you will face. This is where many books on leadership and motivation miss the mark. I can't motivate you. Your motivation has to come from something inside of you. That's why it's called *self*-motivation, not *other*-motivation.

Your reasons why you are doing something have to keep you charged up. The BrickHouse principles and *Always Advance* methodology will help you understand *how* to get things accomplished. But only you can choose *why*.

Life can have a greater meaning than just the day-to-day occurrences common to everyone. You get to choose the meaning of your own life. You get to decide *why*.

"Seemed like a good idea at the time," is not a good reason why. Yet that's how many people justify their days. Spend some time with this and gain some self-awareness around where you're going and why. If you don't, you'll fold up and quit at the first sign of trouble.

The entire BrickHouse Vision Statement package is available in Appendix I. These statements outlined who we would become and who we would serve. Our *whys* were personal. As a team, we weren't required to share them but as a leader, I would talk at length to each member to find out just why they wanted to be a part of BrickHouse. I was particularly interested in people who used the words "being of service" or "bringing joy to others." If I didn't hear that exactly, I could still generally gauge the person's motivation around serving others and being part of a team.

As a leader, it's useful to find out what motivates each individual on your team. You can then better create growth opportunities that will potentially benefit everyone. Being able to fit each person's "micro-agenda" into the band's "macro-agenda" allowed me to reduce turnover and continually improve the product. For the most part, Brooke and I have been able to create the kinds of opportunities that our individuals wanted. And it has been different for each person in the band.

For myself, I wanted the challenge of starting a project from scratch and taking it to the highest level within its given market. This satisfied my competitive nature while also giving me an outlet for my musical talent. Not insignificantly, it also gave my wife and I something to *Always Advance* towards together.

There were other *whys* that would become clearer to me as time went on. I found that I really enjoyed developing people and talent. I enjoyed supporting them, coaching them and building them up. I enjoyed watching them become better performers and hopefully better people. And I liked being in charge of my own destiny. I liked being the *leader*.

But most of all, I liked winning. Yes, that's correct. *I wanted to win*.

Now I hear all of the artists out there hollering, "Sell-out!" They're asking, "Why aren't you working to create something beautiful? Where is that in your *why*? Why aren't you putting the music above everything and letting the rest follow from that? How can you just talk about something as mundane as winning? What about the purity of your art?"

Let me address this because it's very important. First of all, I *do* want to create something beautiful – and I do make the music important. It goes along with producing an outstanding product.

But I'm not doing it simply for my own artistic gratification or for the love of my art. Nor am I doing it because I want adoring fans and glory. *I'm doing it to serve our customers!*

Let me repeat this so that all of the out-of-work musicians, actors, painters, dancers, poets, mimes and spoken word artists who sometimes take themselves too seriously and their audience too lightly can clearly hear it. *I'm doing it to serve our customers!*

The BrickHouse Philosophy says, "Serve the customer and you can stay in the phone book!"

Oops, sorry if I've touched a nerve. But here's the deal plain and simple. My job is to keep our band in the phone book. Without happy customers, there are no gigs. There is no musical fulfillment. There is no art. There is no applause. Customers pay our salary. If you're in the BrickHouse Band, you can think of Brooke and me as your own personal National Endowment for the Arts committee. We're keeping you in the game. But we're only in the game as long as there is a customer willing to pay. The band is "expense." The customer is "revenue." A very wise person once said that all of the money you will ever have in the future is currently in the hands of someone else. That's why we pay attention to a number of issues beyond the music.

In addition to making the music important, we make the equipment, the choreography, the costuming, the lighting, the setup, the venue owners, the agents, the sound engineers, our physical appearance, our marketing materials and every possible peripheral aspect of the business important. This keeps us viable in an incredibly competitive and difficult market.

When you become successful, you can have other people handle many of these peripherals. Delegating some of these details will allow you to more fully concentrate on your art. That's a terrific position to be in. But never delegate control to the extent that you lose *personal touch* with your customers. Walmart founder Sam Walton used to say that there is only one boss, your customer. That customer can fire everyone simply by spending his money somewhere else. Lose touch with your customer and you will not stay successful.

The BrickHouse philosophy contends that "attention equals love." Show us what you pay attention to and we'll show you what you love. Isn't it true that you show your love for your spouse and children when you're paying attention to them? The same holds true for your customer. They can feel it when you pay attention to them and that's when they feel loved. We all want love. So do your customers. Pay attention to them.

Why is this so important? Because everyone trumpets the idea of customer service yet few businesses actually practice it. Customer service should be a given. But at least in the United States, it's not. As such, we've made it a differentiator that has helped us distance ourselves from our competition. Providing great customer service can be difficult and tedious. After all, if it was easy, we'd experience it more often ourselves.

Outstanding customer service requires patience. It requires attention. It requires discipline. It requires that you actually give a damn. But sadly, patience, attention, discipline and giving a damn are qualities seldom practiced any more. In addition, many people now seem to think that serving others is beneath their dignity. But that's great news for us. Why? Because if our competitors are not providing outstanding customer service, *we can! This is an immense competitive advantage that is within our control to deliver!*

Generally, helping others get what *they* (customer) want is the best way to get what *you* want. The fact that this is such a basic lesson, yet so seldom practiced is why we raise it here. We use the acronym PAD-G to remind ourselves that we can gain a competitive advantage with customer service:

P = **Patience** with the customer. Even when they are difficult, be patient.

A = **Attention** that translates to loving our customers and giving them what they want.

D = **Discipline** that is characterized by consistent customer service all the time.

G = **Give a damn!**

Whenever we feel stressed about our performance, or we're not feeling on top of our game, *we bring our attention back to the customer*. We take the focus off of ourselves and put it back where it belongs. How can we help the customers enjoy themselves? How can we make it the most fun for them? How can we serve? Just as in our relationships, taking the spotlight off of ourselves and putting it on the people we care about is the fastest way to ensure success.

I strongly encourage you to understand your customer audience. That requires being engaged with them, listening to them, and yes, loving them. We handle our customers by addressing the following three points.

1. **We ask them what they want.**

   Asking the customer what they want gives you more than just the necessary information around what you need to deliver. It also establishes a relationship. From the basis of that relationship, you can find out exactly what they want in detail. For example, if they are looking for a wedding reception band, we give them a detailed questionnaire. Most brides are very happy to get it because if they have not hired a wedding planner, our questionnaire helps them get organized. In the guise of asking questions, we are also helping to educate them about how most successful weddings work, and what might possibly go wrong.

We ask them what they want for the first dance and for the parent's dance. We find out what special requests they would like us to play from our playlist. We ask them if there are any songs not on the list that they would like us to learn. By special arrangement, we can even have someone in the wedding party come up and sing with us. We also offer them the opportunity to rehearse with us.

In addition, we offer to teach the wedding party special choreography or dance in advance so that they can perform with the band. This always delights their family and friends. We find out what the wedding colors are and we match our costuming to those colors. We provide "master of ceremonies" services where appropriate and a piano bar for their dinner if they choose.

At corporate parties, we'll sometimes bring a dance instructor and give a 15 minute dance lesson before the band begins. These are all "extras" that not a lot of bands offer. We make available these services because we respect our customers and we exist only to serve them. In order to serve them, we must compete to win the jobs they provide – and most of all, we need to know exactly what they want. We pay close attention and listen to what they tell us.

2. We tell them honestly what we can deliver.

In most cases, we can deliver what they want. But occasionally, we'll refer a potential client to a band that is more suited to their needs. We never want to over-promise and under-deliver. For example, we are not a country western band. Sure, we'll do a few country-rock crossover hits but if you are looking for a night of country western music, we are not the band for you. As a result, we'll refer them to a band that might be a better fit. But if we determine that we are the best fit for what they want, which is usually the case, we, or our agent, will draw up a contract. We make our commitment to the customer a personal one. We make sure that they know us and likewise, we make sure that we know them.

There are actually bands that we compete with who are prohibited by their agent from talking with clients before the event. We've had calls from outraged mothers of brides who had already signed contracts with agents figuring they'd get to work out the wedding songs with the band beforehand. They were told that the band would show up at the appropriate date and time and that the wedding party would enjoy what they play. While these are very talented bands, in the BrickHouse world, this is arrogance at the highest level. It is also a complete lack of respect for the people paying you. To be really successful, you must communicate with your customer.

3. **Then we deliver on that contract – and exceed expectations.**

There have been many nights when a corporate dinner ran long. Or perhaps the award ceremony ran overtime. The band was scheduled to play from 8:00 until 11:00 but it is now 9:15 and the band is not yet on stage. Most bands play 50 minute or one hour sets per their contract. Then they take a break and come back for the next set. But that scenario doesn't always serve the customer. Many a night we have played a minimum of two hours with no breaks so that the customer could get what they paid for. In addition, why lose the momentum when everyone is on the dance floor having a great time! They pay us to perform and entertain; not to take breaks.

That's just one example of exceeding expectations. We always strive to deliver more than we promise. Brooke had a great idea that has proven to be a real hit at corporate events. About four songs into the night, our three women singers will rip off their jackets and reveal tops with that particular corporation's name or logo in glitter. The place goes nuts. There are a million little ways you can pleasantly surprise a customer. If you are interested in serving them, you will think of as many as possible.

If we are successful, our customers actually feel like they are a part of our band. They feel like a participant, right there with us all the way. It's a bonding process that begins with the first customer contact – and if we do it well – our relationship will continue long past the time our services are rendered.

Beyond being revenue, customers control your reputation. That's another way of saying that they control just exactly how good you are. In our world, the customers decide if you are an outstanding band. Their perception of you becomes the reality. Whatever they believe becomes the truth. We are only an outstanding band with an outstanding product if the customer says so. In the age of the worldwide web, it's important that they give us that moniker because word travels quickly.

Ultimately, it comes down to this: Understand your customer. Understand your market. Understand what it is you're doing. Understanding these things will be the focus of BrickHouse Principle Number 2 in the next chapter.

Key Points from Chapter One

- Remember the Hippocratic Oath, "Above all, do no harm." If you can't help with something, at least try not to make things worse. Bring solutions, not problems.
- Compete until you win. A loss is just a loss. Big deal. Get up and continue competing.
- The customer is always right. Success is as simple as finding out what customers will pay for and providing it better than anyone else.
- People who are not successful in their lives will probably not be successful in your business. Look thoroughly at their lives and hire quality individuals.
- *Always Advance*. Continually move towards your destination. If you are always going forward, you're always making progress. This is the most certain way to ensure that you compete until you win.
- Know where you are headed and who you want to be. Know your destination. How can you know

you have won if you don't know where you're headed? If you are competing to win, know what winning looks like. Meaningful vision and mission statements will clarify this for you.

- Know *why* you are competing. You must have a compelling reason as to why you are doing anything. Otherwise, you will give up when things get difficult.
- Attention equals love. Pay attention to your customers. Customers control your reputation. Understand them and deliver on your promises.

CRAIG COLEMAN – Guitar and Vocals

Courtesy of Lumina Photography

It is fitting that BrickHouse guitarist Craig Coleman be featured in this chapter. He's a man who has always known where he was going and why. Craig has a deep sensitivity reflected not only in his music, but even more importantly, in his relationships. This sensitivity comes from self-awareness. He knows who he is and why he does what he does.

First and foremost, Craig is a musician. He thinks, feels,

and expresses music. A performer for life, Craig is also an award-winning composer who appreciates every kind of musical genre. This grasp and openness to so many styles of music is not unlike his openness to all types of people. He embraces everyone with a warmth and likeability that has made him an incredibly popular band member with audiences everywhere.

While Craig would admit that he is a perfectionist, he has patience and compassion for those who are not as skilled. These qualities have helped him to become one of the most in-demand musical instructors in the Northwest. In addition, his musical lecture series has become extremely popular and is now featured in the BrickHouse product portfolio. His ability to articulate his thoughts and bring his extraordinary musical experiences to life makes him an invaluable asset to the BrickHouse brand name.

Whether performing one of his signature guitar solos on stage, or recording tracks in the studio, Craig brings outstanding professionalism every time. In a brief question and answer session, Craig shared some of his experiences with BrickHouse.

Q: What unique quality or qualities do you believe have made you successful both in life and in the band?

A: Both in life and in the band, I aspire to be perfect in the tasks that I perform. I take music and performing very seriously. I am very conscientious. I always try to work with the people around me for the greater good. But while often serious, I can remain easy-going and focused while I work. I enjoy feeling a sense of completion and seeing something that was initially intangible turn into something tangible.

Q: What have you learned from your life experience that you've brought to the band?

A: I have learned how to work with people and their different personalities. Management training has also helped me be able to navigate around the psyche of human beings. In living all over the world and experiencing various ethnic cultures, I have found most people to be basically the same. The key is to find the thread that runs through everyone.

Q: What have you learned from your band / music experience that you've taken back into your life?

A: I have a sense of confidence in knowing that I am doing something I am good at.

I am proud to be a working professional musician. In most cultures being an artist is a sacred and life fulfilling journey. I take full responsibility for that journey and all of the fruits and nuts that come with it!

Q: What do you value most about the other members of the band? What have you learned from them?

A: I value many things from being in this band. I particularly enjoy the camaraderie with the members. I have been a professional musician for over 40 years. In many of those situations there have been musicians with idiosyncrasies ranging from mental health issues to alcoholism to delusions of grandeur. The people in BrickHouse are all level-headed, caring and sincere. In addition, they are all true musicians in their own rite. The leaders are competent with their vision. Being a leader myself in another band, I understand what Lee and Brooke deal with. They have validated my own thoughts, ideas and concepts on what makes a band successful.

Q: What is your favorite band memory to this point? Any particularly humorous moment? Painful or embarrassing moment? Educational moment?

A: Oh man, some of these moments should not be expressed in a book! (He laughs.) I do remember one time travelling across the mountains in a band car caravan. Lee drank too much coffee. There were no bathrooms in sight. It was freezing cold outside. The entire caravan stopped once we found a shed Lee could hide behind. Unfortunately for Lee, our sound man brought a camera. You can imagine the rest. It was hilarious.

Q: Do you have a particular philosophy of life that you embrace?

A: Well... It is very simple. Try to live a good life, love the ones you're with, try to have honesty and integrity in all that you do, work hard and "keep rockin!"

CHAPTER 2

Due Diligence: Do Your Homework, Then Play to Your Strengths

BrickHouse Principle Number 2: You must research the market; then do it YOUR way.

"The victor does not believe in chance." Once again I quote Friedrich Nietzsche because he understood the value of doing your homework. Doing your homework does not have to be a drag. You can make it fun. You can have a blast talking and corresponding with people who have been successful doing what you want to do. Preparing for success is exhilarating because you get to learn about how things are done – and then you get to do it YOUR way!

The BrickHouse Philosophy says, "If you fail to prepare, prepare to fail."

Even though it's fun, preparing properly requires patience. Doing your homework means to take care of every possible contingency that could arise. That can take time.

But think of the competitive advantage you're giving yourself. Imagine if Monday through Friday, you worked just fifteen more minutes than your competition. Then imagine if you worked just fifteen minutes more than that. That's two-and-a-half extra hours per week. That may not seem like much but it adds up to 130 hours per year. That's more than three work weeks for the average person. But you're not interested in being average. If you were, you wouldn't be reading this.

Constants

People who take the time to prepare can often succeed against more talented competition. Only you have the final say over how long and how effectively you work and prepare. That is an example of a "constant." Constants are the things that you control. There are certain things that are almost always within your control. How you look, what you say, how you behave, where you go, who you hang out with, where you place your attention, and how you spend your time are generally up to you. Aren't they? If not, send whoever *is* in charge of those things off to the makeover specialist and you'll instantly improve!

Variables

If you take care of the things that are within your power to control, that leaves you free to handle any "variables" that come up. Variables are things over which you have no control. More than likely though, you just didn't think of them. Other than natural disasters, your ability to plan for variables is only limited by your experience and knowing what to look for. After all, you don't know what you don't know. So how can you plan for that?

Great question! That's why we do research. You have to research what could possibly happen. Ask other people in your business about their experiences. Ask them what could possibly go wrong. Even if they are your competitors, they'll probably love sharing stories of their disasters and how they overcame them. They're always funnier in retrospect. Read every book, article and internet blog that you can find for information in your field. Go out and examine what other people are actually producing. Brooke and I scouted bands every weekend for a solid year while we were putting our team together. We needed to know what bands were succeeding and why. Notice I didn't say what bands were *good*. I said what bands were *succeeding*. That's an important distinction. We've seen many excellent bands fold up for a variety of reasons. Some didn't have a plan. Some had personality conflicts that couldn't be overcome. Some had financial problems and some simply didn't have the will to continue when adversity hit.

As we watched the successful bands, we took notes. When possible, we asked them questions whenever they took a break or finished a show. We wrote down every song they played in the order they played it. We noticed what they seemed to care about and what they let slide. We timed how long their sets were. We looked at how they dressed and what they said. We asked them how they got booked. Then we looked at how we could use that information to our benefit. That is the value of research.

But no matter how much research you do, there will always be variables that you didn't anticipate. Examples of variables for a band include: 1) a venue with bad electricity; 2) a wedding ceremony where all rehearsed plans are changed at the last minute, including where the band will set up; 3) an occasion when a member of your band gets ill; 4) a fog machine that sets off the venue's smoke alarm or even 5) an unplanned wardrobe malfunction.

As in all businesses, stuff happens. But with proper preparation, even these potential calamities can be averted. We learned to scout venues in advance. If the venue was far away, we would ask a reputable person at the location to check it out for us. If a band member got ill or was traveling, we had backup musicians trained and ready to go. We took steps to ensure that all of our equipment and costuming was ready and that we had backup systems where needed.

This is where a checklist can be valuable. Having a checklist to consult helps ensure you've planned for any potential variable. For a band, the checklist would cover all of the equipment from the largest speakers to tiny batteries. Do the people in your band have a map to the venue? Do they have contact and emergency phone numbers? We've included a sample checklist in the Appendices for reference.

We've even taken our checklist a step further. We have a detailed map of how the band van will be packed so that everything will fit and no time is wasted trying to cram things into a tight space. Time is precious and proper preparation helps you to save it.

It is imperative that you continue to strive towards eliminating variables. In addition to improving your product, it will eliminate stress. Knowing that you've eliminated problems in advance gives you a sense of confidence that makes everything easier and more fun.

Education

The most effective method of eliminating variables is to become educated. Just as proper preparation begins with research, it continues with education. Your education should be ongoing, never ending, and designed to provide you with useful knowledge. That knowledge will become competitive power when you put it to use. If you are always advancing, you need as much knowledge as you can accumulate.

Our first major educational moment came during our very first band scouting mission. I was completely ignorant as to what had occurred electronically, digitally, and otherwise in all technical aspects of the music industry between the early 1980's and the year 2000. I had no idea as to how music was being produced. There was much to learn.

On that first scouting mission, Brooke and I watched a very popular local cover band. Almost immediately, we noticed some very curious things. On stage were a guitar player, a drummer, a keyboard player and three female singers. There was no bass player, yet we swore we heard a bass guitar. Even more interesting, one of the female singers, a very talented vocalist who has since become a friend of ours, seemed to be singing all of the leads. Her two female colleagues stood on either side of her and provided synchronized choreography. They were singing backup vocals yet sometimes, they were turned completely around with their backs to the microphone. However, this did not seem to affect the volume or quality of the vocals.

How could this be?

Next the band began to play a popular song by the artist Shakira. This particular song features a pan flute at the beginning and end of the song. The keyboardist was not playing during the pan flute part. It wasn't coming from him. Yet the pan flute was there, plain as day. I heard it loud and clear. I looked high and low. There was no pan flute on that stage. I looked around at the patrons on the dance floor. I looked at the people in the audience. Either no one else noticed this or no one cared. But Brooke and I cared. We wanted to know what was going on!

As we looked further, we noticed that the keyboard player had a computer. After the show, we spoke with him and the lead singer. They patiently explained to us about what's come to be known as, "music in the can" or "midi sequencing."

Midi sequencing involves running instruments through tracks on a computer. I knew nothing about it but as Brooke and I continued to scout bands, we noticed that the most successful ones seemed to be doing it. There were a variety of ways to sequence, but the bottom line was, the bands doing the sequencing were packing their venues. They had a bigger sound. They had happy customers. When we talked about midi sequencing to certain musicians, they were outraged. To them, it seemed fake. It allowed a machine to take the place of a human. Why, in their eyes, it was practically immoral.

Was it really immoral? Well, it wasn't immoral to the happy customers who danced the night away. They didn't seem unhappy about paying a lesser or no cover charge to hear the great music the "midi-sequenced bands" were pumping out. These bands were a competitive business success. The customers were charged less. The band made more money because they weren't paying string and horn players. It seemed like a win for everyone. To our way of thinking, it wasn't a question of morality, although many musicians wanted to argue this point. But to an objective observer, it was just competitive business playing itself out in the marketplace.

When Ashlee Simpson had her embarrassing moment on Saturday Night Live, none of us who understood sequencing were surprised. For those who didn't see it, Ashlee began singing a song while a different song with her voice was heard at the same time. Her band stopped playing, the song continued and she exited the stage.

When the wrong song came out of the "can" and she stopped performing, I felt her pain. But the thing is, all of the musicians on that stage were playing – and I'm guessing Ashlee was going to sing along with her prerecorded vocal track. Almost all performances on big stages these days get supplemented. There are additional instruments and often prerecorded vocal tracks being used during live appearances. That's just how it is. I didn't grow up with this technology but if that's the deal now, that's the deal. The customers are demanding perfection. The artists, agents, and sound engineers are trying to provide it.

The bottom line for us was that if we were going to compete in this marketplace, we were going to have to understand this technology. So we hired a local college professor at $110 an hour to come to our house. He taught us everything he could about midi sequencing. He talked. We listened. We implemented. Years later, this ability to provide a fully orchestrated sound has given us a competitive advantage that is hard to beat. We now have the potential for sixteen additional computerized musicians in addition to our drummer, bass player, guitarist and keyboardist. It works wonders and we love it. One of the highlights of my time as a bandleader was when that very keyboardist who explained midi sequencing to me that first night came to see our band. About four years had passed and he told me that our band had surpassed his. He was very gracious to say that. But he was right. And it was an incredibly gratifying moment for me.

Does sequencing sometimes complicate things? Yes. Were there some nightmares implementing it? You bet. Does it require extra work? Always. But sometimes striving to be the best requires extra work. It requires extra research. It requires ongoing education. But in doing a cost-benefit analysis, the benefit we have gained from midi sequencing and the extra work has far outweighed the costs by a long-shot. In addition to a better live performance, it allows us to rehearse with a full band sound when a band member can't attend. It truly gives us a competitive advantage. Without the research and education that our preparation provided us, we could have never succeeded as we have. Proper preparation is critical to any business success.

I should also mention that The BrickHouse Band has never used prerecorded vocal tracks but we are not opposed to it. Why? Because I care only about giving customers a product they want. If there is anything that will give us a competitive advantage in the future, I'll be open to trying it.

Context

In chapter one, we talked about having vision and mission statements. We drafted our vision and mission at the same time we were researching the market. This made perfect sense because we needed to know more about our market before we could make an educated decision on how to attack it. All we knew when we began was that we wanted to start a band and we wanted to play on that huge casino stage. So we drafted our vision, mission and goals while we learned. Then we simply adjusted accordingly as we learned more about what we'd gotten ourselves into. This leads us to "context."

Context is another way of saying "your situation." At certain times in my life I've believed myself to be in a duck pond – only to find out it was actually a shark tank. While I'm speaking metaphorically, this sums up a number of business situations I've jumped into because I hadn't done the proper research. I hadn't understood the context within which I was operating. I had abdicated my responsibility and simply trusted other people to know what they were doing. It was an expensive lesson. You need to be personally satisfied that you understand the context and environment of any business situation you enter. You must take complete personal responsibility for knowing everything you need to know. Like Oprah always says, "Sign your own checks."

Back in the early 1980's, not long after graduating from Illinois State University, I took a job at a business college in suburban Seattle. This was about the time that word processing was introduced as all the rage. Our college taught word processing on Xerox and Wang computers. We also taught accounting and some fundamental computer programming. The courses were great and the facilities were clean and professional. The instructors were mostly young people like me. This was cost effective because, just out of college, they were not yet demanding huge salaries. Things seemed to be going well and we were having success getting people into jobs after taking our classes.

My job was to oversee marketing materials, enroll students and help place them into jobs within the business community. I also acted as the dean for any student concerns that arose. All in all, it was very satisfying. And while I worked extremely long hours, I enjoyed the feeling of success it gave me.

There was however, one problem. I was not aware of it because I had not done my homework. I became aware of it the first time one of my paychecks bounced. Before I took the job, I had not examined the college's financial situation and the context within which they were operating. I was young and I just trusted that because everything looked good, it was good. But that was not the case.

If you were around in the early 1980's, you may recall that there was a huge savings and loan scandal. As it turned out, our college had all of our receivables being collected by a local savings and loan. In reality, what little they were bothering to collect was not going anywhere near our coffers. After much struggle, we tried to sue for our receivables but we did not have the financial resources for a long legal battle. It would not have mattered. The entire savings and loan industry folded. Unfortunately, we folded as well.

Had I done a little homework before getting involved,

I could have saved myself considerable time, effort and money. With a little research, I could have found out that we were not collecting receivables and that the financial outlook was bleak. The lesson here is to simply look at the "context" around and within which you are operating. For a band, that means looking at how many venues might potentially hire you. It means looking at what they pay. It means finding out what they want and when you would perform. It means looking at performing for fairs and festivals. It means looking at your competition to find out how talented they are and what they're doing that sells. It means talking to booking agents and anyone connected with hiring.

But when talking to booking agents, it also means being careful what you say. Brooke has also been guilty of thinking she was in a duck pond while talking with a shark. First of all, let me say, there are many wonderful booking agents out there. In fact, we probably could not have survived without them. And in our experience, there are more good ones than bad. But one wrong thing said to a mean-spirited agent can undermine years of hard work.

We had just been booked for a week headlining a major northwest casino. It was a Tuesday through Saturday gig and it was something we had worked for since we began. It was a milestone achievement in our growth and we were excited. Before taking it on, Brooke wanted to get us a couple of tune-up shows at some small restaurant-bars. This would allow us to try some new material and fine-tune the show. So she called a local booking agency. Brooke knew the gentleman who ran this agency. She also knew that he did not have a sterling reputation. He drank too much; he talked too much and much of what came out of his mouth was not kind. When we first began, other musicians told us to be careful around him. He was known to be less than honest in his dealings with bands and club owners. But he controlled some of the smaller venues in the northern Seattle suburbs and you had to go through him to play them. We didn't care about making money on these shows. We just wanted to try some new material in a live setting. Brooke figured, "What could it hurt?"

As it turned out, it hurt a lot. This agent was surprised to hear from Brooke because our band rarely played these kinds of venues any more. He asked her why she wanted to do these small clubs. Innocently, Brooke explained that we had been booked for a week at the large casino. Hearing this, the agent became angry. Turns out, he had been trying to get his top band in there for three years with no success. He was outraged. *The very next day, we were cancelled at that casino.* Someone had called and said that there was a problem with us. It could not have been a coincidence. We are certain that he called them and heaven only knows what he told them. He might have told them that we were drug-addled, no talent bums who kept dead bodies in our van. We'll never know for certain. But this is an example of how you must understand the context within which you are operating. Be careful what you say and to whom you are speaking. Be careful what you do. It's not a duck pond out there.

This was a particularly painful lesson because it was one major factor in four people getting discouraged and leaving our band. You see, it's not all a glamorous bed of roses and they couldn't handle the loss. It took time to regroup. But by the time this setback had occurred, we had embraced the methodology of *Always Advance*. As a result, we traded up in those four positions and became better than ever. In the long run, it actually worked out for the best. But it took valuable time.

Learning about context is critical for your team members as well. I once heard a story about a famous college basketball coach. He was concerned that his team didn't have a clue about the context within which they were operating. Immediately after a game one night, he gave each of his players a piece of paper. He asked them to write the answers to the following questions.

1. What was the score of the game we just played?
2. What was the score of the game we played last week?
3. What is our team's record (how many wins and losses)?
4. Who is our next opponent?
5. Where are we in our conference standings? (1st, 2nd, 3rd, etc.)

He was aghast to find out that many of his players could not correctly answer any of these questions. He realized that he needed to help his team understand these contextual questions so that they could grasp the importance of where they were in relation to the competition. Why? Because the context of your situation can often determine your strategy.

It's the same in business. We all need to know where we stand. We need to know who the competition is and what the score is. Are we winning or losing? How much time is left? These are critical to know in order to design and implement an effective strategy.

As a Certified Public Accountant, Brooke has sometimes contracted to work with small business owners who had no idea of what their own financial situation was. They had no idea of the context under which they were operating. How could they make intelligent business decisions without even knowing how much money they had? Just as important, how could they make intelligent decisions if they didn't know whether they were making a profit and what their financial trend was in relation to their own history and that of their competitors?

Some self-proclaimed business experts will argue that you simply need to concentrate on what *you* are doing without worrying about anything or anyone else. When it comes to performing a task, I agree. But you need to understand context in order to know that you are working on the right things. Your strategy involves knowing what to do and why you are doing it. You can only get that from understanding context. As such, understanding context is a vital part of proper preparation.

Remember, doing your homework will minimize unwanted surprises down the road. As a summary to this section, here are some questions that can help you do your homework properly.

Why are you getting into this business? What is your most compelling reason?

How will you know when you are successful?

At this point, who do you believe your customer will be?

What job are you going to be hired to do? (Look deeply because it may not be what you think.)

What are the successful people in your business doing? Can it be replicated?

What are the people who are struggling in my business doing? Can I ensure that I'm not doing those things?

What kind of financing do I need and what do I already have?

Who are my allies in this?

Who might try to thwart this effort, either intentionally or unintentionally?

How many employees do I need and what characteristics do they need in order to be successful?

How can I maximize our strengths and minimize our weaknesses?

How can I differentiate my product and stand out from everyone else in the market?

What is my detailed plan to implement this product?

Do I have the will to see this through to completion?

We'll continue to help you answer a number of these questions as we travel further.

The BrickHouse Philosophy says, "Know who your REAL customer is."

During my early years in the aerospace business, I took a class called "World Class Competitiveness." It was an excellent class if for no other reason than it taught me the value of using reliable and repeatable processes for producing a product. More importantly, it taught me the value of customer knowledge. As we alluded to earlier, having an intimate and detailed knowledge of your customer is useful in any business.

However, the class made one fundamental error. It identified the customer as the next person in the chain of a process that receives your product. I completely disagreed and still do. In the BrickHouse world, *your customer is the person who pays you.* If you can find out what the person who signs your check wants, you have a shot at succeeding.

For example, as a band, we will occasionally play high-end wedding receptions. It would be easy to assume that our customers are simply the people on the dance floor. If they are happy, we've done our job, right? Not necessarily. They are certainly important. In fact, anyone who is touched by your product is important. But they are only secondary customers. Their importance lies in the fact that their reaction to our product may well influence our primary customer. Why? Because it is our primary customer that is paying us. In this case, the primary customer is generally the mother and father of the bride. If they are happy, we have satisfied our customer. After all, at the end of the day, they are generally the ones writing the check.

You also cannot assume that you understand what the customer wants or what their agenda is. For example, many casinos want bands to take a thirty minute break every hour. When we began, that seemed insane to us. You mean, we spend an hour building up the energy of the place and filling the dance floor only to stop just when it gets going?

Yes. That's exactly the case. Why? Because unlike a corporate party where they would prefer minimal breaks, the casino is not making money while people are dancing. They are making money when the people on the dance floor go gamble in the casino. So yes, they want to break the energy and momentum we've worked so hard to create. Once again, it's not about the band. It's never about us. It's always about the customer.

The lesson here is that you can't assume that you know who your real customer is. And you certainly can't assume that you know what's best for them. They will tell you what they want. Ask them what ultimate victory looks like for them. Listen to them. Then deliver. Help them win – and you'll be victorious as well.

The BrickHouse Philosophy says, "Your travel plan should include D-S-M-F: Destination-Situation-Map-Fuel."

By now, you probably understand that we are on a journey. This journey is about taking an idea, no matter how outrageous or impractical, and turning it into a reality. And every successful journey requires certain fundamental essentials. You have already been introduced to some of the components of these fundamental essentials. They are your vision, mission and an understanding of the context within which you are operating. By themselves, these things are great to know. However, in order for you to turn an idea into a substantive reality, they need to be integrated into an organized plan.

For planning, the BrickHouse philosophy uses the initials D-S-M-F. These stand for Destination, Situation, Map and Fuel. Together they constitute the fundamental essentials you need for traveling anywhere. If you are taking your family on a vacation, you need to know where you're going (destination), the circumstances surrounding the trip (situation), and how to get there (map). You also need the right kind and amount of fuel (resources). You need these same essentials when you go on a business journey.

Your destination is clarified within your vision and mission. If you have looked at the context and circumstances you're in, you understand your situation. Your map will serve as your route or plan for getting to the destination. Your fuel represents what you need in order to execute your plan.

Fundamental Essentials for Your Journey

DESTINATION = Vision and Mission

SITUATION = Context

MAP = Route/Plan

FUEL = Resources Necessary to Execute Your Journey

It's mind-boggling that a business would not operate from a plan. Yet some don't. You don't hear much about them because they quickly disappear. Brooke and I have watched people with far more talent than us fail simply because they had no plan. Without a plan, you can't survive no matter how talented you are. Sometimes a business will begin with a plan and forget to refer to it as they get "caught up" in other activities. The trouble with this is that when you move away from your plan, you sometimes forget what your original destination was. And you end up on the road to somewhere else.

Destination

Your destination is the most important fundamental essential to remember in the D-S-M-F formula. That's why it comes first. It should drive everything that you do. Your destination is your number one priority and it represents your ultimate desired outcome. *It represents results.* If you are always advancing and competing to win, you'll know you've won when you reach your destination.

If life is a journey, you must always refer back to your destination. Where are you going? Asking that question keeps you centered on what's important. If you begin to get confused, always ask, "What is my destination? Where am I going?" Perhaps the most important question you can ever ask is, *"Is what I'm doing now advancing me towards my destination?"* This will clarify your desired outcome and bring you back to the most important thing. If what you're doing is not advancing you towards the destination, you must ask yourself why you are doing it.

Because your destination is your number one priority, it requires your sustained attention. You cannot allow distractions. The shortest distance to any destination is a straight line. You can't afford too many turns along the way. Every turn you take is simply a distraction keeping you from getting results. Keep your attention on where you are headed. Look at it. See it. Feel it. In fact, feel free to be obsessive about it. *Always Advance* towards your destination and you will eventually arrive.

Getting everyone in your organization to sign on to your destination is critical to your success. If your destination is New York but two of your colleagues would rather go to Phoenix, there will be problems. These disagreements and conflicts must be resolved, or else personnel must be changed.

Brooke and I once had a situation where two of our female members lost sight of the destination. Our destination was to be a Vegas-style showband with attractive people, stylish costuming and "current" choreography that entertained young and old alike. At the time, there were no bands in the Seattle area fitting this description. As a result, this vision was critical to differentiating our band from others. Our two female members at the time decided that another destination would be more to their liking. They stated that they would only wear slacks at shows and that the choreography should be more like that of the "60s Supremes" era. Anything resembling hip-hop or current choreography was just not going to do. They believed that quality vocals would be the key to success.

Brooke practically swallowed her tongue. These ladies didn't want to "offend" any women in the audience by being more attractive than them. Thus, the slacks. I also suspect that they didn't want to spend too much time worrying about their appearance. In addition, they had just seen the movie *Showgirls* and had been influenced by the simplicity of the 60's-style dance moves. They thought this would be preferable to spending hours in a dance studio learning contemporary choreography. Finally, they didn't understand that practically all bands have quality vocals. That's a given. Without costuming and the most current dance moves, we'd be just another bar band.

Our destination was a place beyond what these women could see. This was a shame because they were very capable singers. But it was our responsibility to ensure that they understood and accepted the destination – and they didn't. They decided to exercise their preference and we wished them well as they went off into musical oblivion.

You can't compromise on the destination. Brooke has been stronger about this than I have and she has been right. Worrying about offending people is your ticket to mediocrity. I'm not suggesting you go out of your way to offend anyone, *but you don't have to apologize for being outstanding*. You don't have to apologize for being talented and attractive. I would rather anyone offended by my attempt to be outstanding not be my customer. We're hunting for bigger game. If people are offended by that, I don't want them around me. They will not be my customer. And they will certainly not be in my employ. Why? Because outstanding customers want to associate with outstanding products. Why aspire to anything less.

While your vision and mission outline your ultimate destination, it's true that you will have a number of stops along the way. In fact, these are necessary stops. These are your interim destinations. On your way to your ultimate destination, you should have daily, weekly, monthly and perhaps even yearly interim destinations.

For example, it's unlikely that you would have the stamina to drive from Chicago to Seattle without stopping. Besides, that wouldn't be safe. You'll need to refuel your car. You'll need to refuel yourself with sleep and food. You might want to stop and celebrate on your journey with some sightseeing. To the extent possible, every journey should be celebrated and enjoyed.

Each stop is an important interim destination on the way to Seattle. If you *Always Advance* in the direction of Seattle, eventually you'll see Mt. Rainier in the distance. You'll know you are almost there. And finally, you'll have arrived, one interim destination at a time.

Any goal that you want to achieve, large or small, can be looked at as a destination. If you have to make a sales call, what is your ultimate destination with that call? Where are you going with it? What is your desired outcome? Are you trying to close on an appointment? Are you trying to make the sale right there on the phone? If you always know what the destination is, you are more likely to get there. It requires a commitment to sustained attention on what you're doing. It requires a commitment to your most important priority.

Brooke and I laugh about what we call the "shiny object" syndrome. It refers to every small or large distraction that takes your attention away from your destination. One of us will be working on something and then out of nowhere..."Oh look, a shiny object! That's interesting. Let's see what it is!"

We laugh because we know we've just been "had" once again. I might be doing research on the internet and see something interesting (shiny object). I click on that and the next thing you know I'm reading a story about Jessica Simpson's latest love interest. While no doubt entertaining, it has nothing to do with getting to my destination.

A recent study referred to in the September, 2009 issue of *Success Magazine* illustrates how distractions have become a way of life. In the study, researchers from the University of California-Irvine followed thirty-six managers and leaders from the business community. They found that the average amount of time spent on a single task before being interrupted or switching tasks was only three minutes. *Three minutes!*

At the end of the day, only results matter. If you didn't reach your destination for the day, don't lie to yourself about how busy you were. Don't excuse yourself because you had too many interruptions. Simply figure out what you need to do differently. Maybe you need to isolate yourself. Maybe you need to stop worrying about being perfect; sometimes getting something done that is "fit for use" is enough. Maybe you need to readjust your schedule.

Remember, winning is all about reaching your destination. There is no substitute. The difference between victory and defeat will ultimately come down to your ability to commit sustained attention to your task. You must eliminate distractions. That will be the key to your success.

Situation

Once you are clear on your destination, you will need to evaluate your current situation. You need to be completely realistic about what resources you have, what resources you'll need, and what actions you'll need to take to bridge the gap between the two. You'll need to fully grasp who you are, who your customers are, and who your competition is.

We knew that our destination for the BrickHouse Band was captured in our vision and mission. Our vision was "to be the northwest's preferred provider of music and entertainment for corporate events, private parties, casinos and weddings." In order to be this, we would have to "provide sensational value by bringing high-energy, interactive, quality entertainment and outrageous fun to all customers."

In order to reach our destination, we evaluated our situation. Any business can do the same. As objectively, honestly and realistically as possible, we answered the following questions.

What kinds of skills and talents do we currently have?

What kinds of skills, talents and people will we need to reach our destination?

What technology and equipment do we currently have that we can use?

What technology and equipment do we need in order to reach our destination? (For example; instruments, microphones, microphone stands and cords, wireless equipment, speakers and monitors, in-ear monitors, sound boards, snakes, computers, smart cards, lighting, costuming, etc.)

What kind of financing do we currently have that can be allocated?

What kind of financing will we need to reach our destination?

What kind of rehearsal facilities will we need that are available?

Of course, these questions led to more questions. But these are the basic questions that businesses have to answer in some form. Skills, talents, equipment, money and facilities must be evaluated.

Also recognize that as you bring more people into your business, you bring in more variables. Things like scheduling and personalities come into play. In putting a band together, you also have to adjust for the fact that until you begin making money, you are essentially dealing with volunteers. It's much more difficult to hold volunteers "accountable." Many civic organizations find themselves in the same situation. After all, these people are not being paid. As a leader, it takes a great deal of emotional intelligence to hold this kind of situation together. You'll learn more about developing the skills of emotional intelligence in chapter four.

Map

The next fundamental essential on your journey is your map. Once you know your destination and your situation, you need a plan that will take you from where you are to where you want to go. That plan is outlined on your map. Your map serves as your business plan and will provide the route that you'll take.

If you know where you are headed, the means to get there will often become obvious. That's why you should review your destination every day. What you need to do and how you need to do it will often become apparent if you simply know where you're going. Your map should include the time, costs and all of the elements identified in your situation that need to be incorporated. Once you've planned your route in detail, you can advance confidently towards the destination.

You can think of your map as a global positioning system (GPS). Brooke has a GPS device in her car. She loves it because it gives the precise route to her destination. It keeps her from veering off in the wrong direction. The map to your destination should perform a similar service.

If you are a romantic spirit, or just easily distracted, you may be tempted by many attractive twists and turns along your route. Beware the "shiny object." Again, stop and ask, "Where am I going? What is my destination?" Always come back to that or you will end up somewhere else. Follow your GPS. It will keep you from these unnecessary detours.

Now, you may accidentally take a wrong turn and it could have a serendipitous effect. That is, you might find yourself in a great place and you might enjoy that very much. But it's not the destination you committed to. It is not the result you are holding yourself accountable for. And if you have people depending on you to reach your committed destination, you may have some explaining to do when you call to tell them you're somewhere else having a grand time.

It could be that you've been thrown off course for any number of reasons. If you find yourself off the map, simply take the fastest path back to your planned route and once again begin advancing towards your destination. It doesn't have to be complicated. In fact, it's better if it's not. Remember, the shortest distance between two points is a straight line. Consult your map and destination often. If you do, you'll *Always Advance* in the right direction.

Fuel

When you looked at your situation, you evaluated the requirements you would need for your journey. These requirements constitute your fuel. They will be different for every business. But some things are constant. Equipment, facilities, capital, and personnel all figure into business success. The best equipment is only as good as the people who run it. The best people will struggle if their equipment is poor. Strive to get the best of both. Shortcuts don't work in the long run.

Anything that you can do to develop the people you work with is worthwhile. People fuel your business. They are the bridge between your product and your customer. Great people can make up for a lack of facilities, equipment and capital. Help your people grow while you grow your business. The more training and education they get, the better off your business will be. Even if they eventually leave, it's the right thing to do – and you'll get a reputation as someone who cares about your employees.

We recognize that our band members need to grow. That sometimes means that they need to go off and play with other people. Our musicians have skills far beyond the funk, rock and top 40 songs we play. They are skilled in everything from big band and swing to polka. So as long as it doesn't interfere with our schedule, our band members are encouraged to go play in other projects from time to time. It contributes to their skill level and their growth. It also gives them joy – and Brooke and I want that for them.

Finally, when you have determined your destination, situation, map and fuel, your fundamental essentials are in place. Now you must execute. You must take action. You must GO!

As you find yourself succeeding, make your successes repeatable by documenting what works. Keep copious records. Document what does not work as well. A short pencil or tiny computer chip is better than a long memory.

Record everything; write it down.

If you have information that is proprietary, keep it protected. Even in the band business, there are proprietary secrets that provide competitive advantages. Our midi sequences and customer knowledge are extremely valuable. Because we compete to win, we keep this information protected.

The BrickHouse Philosophy says, "Don't model their product; make them want to model yours."

Brooke and I continued to scout bands even after assembling our musicians. We would often take our band members with us. However, this came with some risk. If we saw a band whose strengths were vocal harmonies, our band would become enamored with that. They would then want to become the best "vocal harmony" band. Next week we might see a band with a certain play list that worked. Invariably, our band would want to adopt that play list, even if our talents weren't suited to those types of songs. It seemed that our band members were deeply influenced by the "flavor of the week." I could see that I had to get them off of what other people were doing and back to *our* destination.

On the one hand, I wanted them to learn from what worked for others. I also wanted them to be inspired and want to get better. However, I didn't want them to be intimidated by these other bands. And I particularly didn't want them to forget what we did well. It was important that we concentrate on our own strengths. After all, we didn't need to be good at *their* strengths; *we simply needed to be outstanding at ours*.

This situation reminded me of what my late father, who was a basketball coach, used to say. "Never play alley ball with the boys from the alley." He was telling me that instead of getting sucked into doing what others were strong at, you should do things your way. *Play to your own strengths and make the other guys adjust to you!*

In an environment where you have almost total control over your product, it's far more productive to maximize your strengths than to shore up weaknesses. Sure, there will always be areas to improve upon. But sometimes you can simply leave the weaknesses behind. How? *By not doing the things you're weak at!*

Perhaps most importantly, I had to remind our band that our strengths were differentiating us from all the other bands. And we were continuing to improve and build upon those strengths. Playing to our strengths also came with the added advantage of built-in confidence. People are far more assertive in their approach and execution of anything when they are confident. And I wanted our team to adopt that confident mindset. I tried to instill in them the idea that soon, these same other bands would be coming to watch us. When they did, they'd want to emulate what we were doing.

With this mindset, we could begin to set the standard for success. We could become the band everyone else aspired to be.

Strengths

A number of years ago, an author named Joe Hyams was studying martial arts under the legendary Bruce Lee. Joe was complaining about growing older. He told Bruce that he could no longer perform the high kicks that he used to practice when sparring. He went on and on about how frustrating it was to be growing older and less capable.

Bruce would have none of it. Bruce explained that instead of grumbling about the things he could no longer do, Joe should put his attention on the things he still could. In other words, he encouraged Joe to play to the strengths he still had.

As humans, we all have strengths. We also have weaknesses. In order to be successful, it's useful to honestly assess what those strengths and weaknesses are. Looking at our talents, skills, abilities, and shortcomings gives us a sense of who we are and where we stand in the present. It's important to assess ourselves without false modesty on the one hand, or fear of being seen as inferior on the other. It amounts to simply being objective. Don't stress about this. It's perfectly natural to be good at some things and not as good at others. What doesn't seem natural is our ability to tell the difference between the two. Perhaps this is best expressed in the old adage, "We all want what we can't have."

Look around. Singers want to be athletes. Athletes want to be movie stars. Bankers want to be lawyers. And lawyers wonder why they didn't go to medical school. There is a tendency among people to want to be good at something that they are not currently doing and are probably not naturally suited for.

Now I'm not going to be the one to tell you what you can't do. I believe that you can do far more than you probably believe. We all have a certain genetic potential. It's up to you to push the envelope on anything you want to attempt. Those of us practicing the BrickHouse philosophy are all about helping people reach the upper limits of their genetic potential – physically, intellectually, emotionally and artistically. And you'll never know what that potential is if you don't make the attempt.

Having said that, let's stop for a moment. There are a number of well-meaning coaches, trainers and teachers out there who want you to succeed. Like me, they believe you are far more capable than you know. *But there are also some folks out there who will tell you anything you want to hear.* They understand that people want what they can't have. Beware of those people.

Brooke once took modeling classes at a school for aspiring models. While not really interested in modeling as a career, she was interested in improving the way she carried herself. It also allowed her to pick up the latest makeup and fashion tips of the times. However, she winced as she watched school enrollment officials tell wide-eyed young women that with a little training, they could be supermodels. Even to the untrained eye, it was fairly obvious that these girls would never meet the stringent height, weight and appearance requirements of a supermodel. But the girls wanted to believe – and their parents wanted to believe. So they were willing to pay the modeling school a lot of money. Not surprisingly, the modeling school was very willing to accept their generosity.

I certainly don't want to burst anyone's bubble. Hey, go for it! I'm just encouraging you to be smart. There is always someone out there willing to take your money. That's why you need to be objective in your self-assessment. Here's a case in point. I would have loved to have been a professional athlete. I grew up playing a number of sports. I loved football, basketball and tennis like nothing else. But my real talent was in music. Still, I believed that if I just worked hard enough, I could play in the NFL or the NBA. I wasn't objective in my assessment. Instead of putting time and effort into music, I went after sports with unbridled enthusiasm. I practiced hour upon hour and became quite proficient in a number of skills. And this allowed me to take my athletic career farther than I ever could have had I not worked so hard. But at a certain point, I had to recognize that for me, being a professional athlete just wasn't in the cards. Don't get me wrong, I enjoy stories of people who seem to have beaten the odds. But be careful, sometimes the odds aren't quite what they seem.

For example, at the 2009 NBA Slam Dunk contest, the winner was Nate Robinson. Nate stands only about 5 feet and 7 inches tall. As a result, the motivational gurus started pointing and shouting, "See? It's possible! If Nate can do it, *you* can do it! Nate beat the odds! He's small, he plays in the NBA and he won the slam dunk contest!"

Listen, Nate didn't beat any odds. I watched Nate grow up in Seattle. In fact, I watched his father Jacques play football at the University of Washington and be the MVP of the 1982 Rose Bowl. (Are you seeing the genetic potential here?) Nate Robinson is *gifted* in athletics. He played both football and basketball in college. You have to be an amazing athlete to do that at a major college. As a sophomore, he decided to specialize in basketball. But in fact, several NFL scouts still believe he would be a better NFL cornerback than NBA guard. Having watched Nate play since he was a teenager, I would have been amazed had he *not* been a professional athlete. Of course he worked hard and has made the most of his talent. I'm not diminishing his effort in the least. I'm just pointing out that while some people would tell you that Nate overcame the odds, I'm telling you that Nate was simply playing to his strengths. He was smart and correct in objectively assessing his personal assets. He didn't even have to play his senior year at Washington before being drafted into the NBA. He came out of school early and he has succeeded.

If I haven't convinced you yet, I'll refer you to the popular television show, American Idol. Have you ever watched the first few weeks of that show? That's when they travel around showing the thousands of people who audition. Have you listened to some of those auditions? Now I understand that some of that is put on for television. But really, let's be honest, some of those nice people just cannot sing. Am I telling them not to sing? No, no, no – not at all. I would encourage them to enjoy music and sing to their heart's content. What I *am* telling them is that the chances are very great that they will not be professional singers. And seriously, how can they not know this? Are they in complete denial? Do they not hear themselves? It all goes back to, "We all want what we can't have." It all goes back to not objectively assessing strengths and weaknesses.

Are there ever exceptions? You bet. In chapter three, I'll tell you about Henry Rollins. By his own admission, Henry can't sing a lick. Yet he's sold a number of records with the punk band Black Flag and his own Rollins Band. So yes, *it can be done*. Maybe you'll be that exception to the rule. I'd love it if you were. I'm just asking you to become aware of your personal strengths and talents as you pursue your dreams. Doing this allows you to succeed by doing things *your* way.

You may believe that the preceding paragraphs run contrary to this book's theme. In fact, they do not. Yes, this book is about creating something from nothing and doing it against the odds. *But it's also about being smart.* When Brooke and I looked at starting a band, we objectively and accurately assessed our strengths and weaknesses. We believed in each other's musical strengths. I was already skilled as a pianist and had years of experience as a singer (strength). I'd be horrible at fixing a car (weakness) so I let someone else do that. Brooke had several years behind her in dance, theater, and as a karaoke host. She had a four octave vocal range and had been trained in music. If both of us had been tone deaf, we would have applied our energies elsewhere. But believing that we were capable, confident and successful people, we understood that we could handle the music portion of the business.

Where we knew it would get tricky was in all of the other obstacles that we had to address. Age, time, recent musical experience, parenting, careers, handling other musicians, and a host of other issues were barriers that we had to overcome. But everyone has barriers to overcome – even when you play to your strengths. Just how we overcame ours and how you can overcome yours is the subject of the next chapter.

Key Points from Chapter Two

- Doing your homework means to prepare properly and take care of any contingencies that may come up. The victor does not believe in chance.
- People who take the time to prepare will often succeed against more talented competition.
- Constants are the things that you control. How you look, what you say, how you behave, where you go, who you hang out with, where you place your attention, and how you spend your time are generally under your control. Take charge of them.
- Variables are things over which you have no control. By thoroughly researching your business and educating yourself, you can minimize variables.
- It is critical that you understand the context within which you are operating. Understanding the situation and what is going on around you will save you time and money in the long run.
- For planning, we use the initials D-S-M-F. They stand for Destination, Situation, Map and Fuel. Together they constitute the fundamental essentials you need for traveling anywhere.
- Always ask, "Is what I'm doing now advancing me towards my destination?"
- When possible, differentiate yourself from the competition by playing to your strengths. Accentuate and capitalize on the things you do well. Leave your weaknesses behind.

NICOLE STEWART – Vocals and Dance

Courtesy of Lumina Photography

We feature Nikki Stewart in the chapter on "doing your homework" because no one has worked harder or prepared more thoroughly than Nikki. As a result, she has become one of the west coast's most talented and coveted vocalists. In fact, as a result of her work ethic, she has become a "10" in every performance category.

Because she is so "easy on the eyes," people sometimes assume that everything has come easily for her. Not necessarily. While blessed with a terrific voice, Nikki has become an extraordinary dancer through training and practice. She has separated herself from the pack by spending hours in the dance studio. As an adjunct to this, she keeps herself in prime physical condition through a disciplined exercise regimen. Up at 4:30 every morning, Nikki works full time as a dental hygienist before rehearsing every evening on some facet of her performance.

This dedication to preparation has made her the most consistent and outstanding vocalist that BrickHouse has ever featured. Her professional approach inspires everyone to work harder. No one would ever guess that Nikki has also worked to overcome serious stage fright. But she is a living example of what you can accomplish by facing your fears. Perhaps most importantly, she is one of the nicest people you'll ever meet. You never hear a negative word about Nikki. The only negative is that the rest of us in the band have to constantly field questions like, "Who's the gorgeous blonde? Can I talk to her?"

Somehow, we don't mind those questions. We understand why they ask and if you see her, you will too. Nikki Stewart is a name to remember. You'll be hearing a lot more from her.

Our Q & A with Nikki gives you a sense of why we love her.

Q: What unique quality or qualities do you believe have made you successful both in life and in the band?

A: I believe that continually striving for improvement

is essential to achieving success in all aspects of life. My father instilled a strong work ethic in me when I was very young. I come from a blue-collar, single income family. My father worked 12 to 14 hour days even before I was born to provide for our family. He taught me to put my best efforts into everything I do. After years of working full-time as a dental office manager and taking classes at night, I maintained a 4.0 grade point average in college and completed my dental hygiene education. I love being a dental hygienist! Likewise, I've been fortunate to become a member of The BrickHouse Band. It has allowed me to work on becoming a better singer, dancer and all-around entertainer. Singing is my passion – and I'm going to focus on continuously expanding my knowledge and skills.

Q: What have you learned from your life experience that you've brought to the band?

A: Life is short so enjoy every moment. Life has not always been easy for me. I survived a recent divorce from a man who controlled me for fifteen years. He gambled away every dime I had and was unfaithful as well. I've survived having to begin a new life on my own and I've been discovering who I really am and how strong I can actually be. However, the most important thing I've learned is to focus on the positive things and people in my life. I am now starting to relax and enjoy my new life. Life is so much less stressful when you live one day at a time. I work to accomplish the goals I set for each day and then adapt new goals for tomorrow.

Q: What have you learned from your band / music experience that you've taken back into your life?

A: My self-confidence has grown enormously! For ex-

ample, I used to tremble from head to foot when trying to speak or sing in front of others. Now I'm excited to entertain and connect with others. I realize my own value, not only as a singer and entertainer, but as a person as well. I believe it was no accident that I bumped into Lee and Brooke at a karaoke bar years ago. It was a life-changing event that helped me gain the courage to face my own insecurities and take charge of my own destiny. My role in the band has totally changed me and I'm so grateful for that!

Q: What do you value most about the other members of the band? What have you learned from them?

A: I admire everyone in this band for a variety of reasons. Everyone carries a passion and devotion to succeed that inspires me greatly. I truly appreciate the selflessness of each member. I love the support and acceptance I receive; not only in the music-related aspects, but in the advice and guidance I've received around life issues as well. The other members have been musicians for most of their lives, and their technical knowledge of musical theory is amazing!

Q: What is your favorite band memory to this point? Any particularly humorous moment? Painful or embarrassing moment? Educational moment?

A: One my favorite memories of the band is our performance at the Seattle Westin Hotel for the Noevir National Convention. The staging, lighting and professionalism from all involved were phenomenal. But it was the crowd that made it so special. They danced all night long and showered us with love. The compliments and hugs we received afterwards made it a truly great night.

The most humorous, painful and embarrassing moment involved a wardrobe malfunction. Being a very petite woman, sometimes I look for a way to fill out my tops, if you know what I mean. One night at a casino show, the girls wore bikini tops covered by a mesh shirt. While singing and dancing to my first vocal lead of the night, one of the gel inserts to my top began drifting down towards my stomach. I carefully pinned it to my body with my arm, while continuing to sing and dance our choreographed moves (one-handed now). At one point, I turned my back to the audience and tried to shove the insert back into place. This was right in front of our drummer Dale. Then I confidently flipped back around to finish the song. However, I had pushed a little too hard and now the insert was sticking out of the top of the bikini. As if that wasn't enough, the left insert began drifting down. Luckily, the song ended and I ran off the stage. I threw the inserts on the floor, stomped on them and vowed never to wear "falsies" again!

Q: Do you have a particular philosophy of life that you embrace?

A: I believe in the philosophy of "Do unto others as you would have done unto you." I make an effort to treat everyone with the respect, love and support that they deserve. Furthermore, I enjoy working hard and giving more of myself that what is expected, both in my role with the BrickHouse team, and in my job as a hygienist. This philosophy has always served me well.

CHAPTER 3

The Last Band Standing: Cultivate the Skill, the Chill and the Will

BrickHouse Principle Number 3: You must be competent, courageous and resolute.

As I write this, the United States is in a very serious economic recession. It seems as if everyone is running scared. People are worried about the economy. They're afraid they will lose their homes. Or they're afraid they'll lose their jobs. When they're not worrying about the economy, they're worrying about something else. They're worried about being too fat, or that they'll never be loved, or that they'll never get what they want.

The BrickHouse philosophy suggests that there are only three things that keep people from ever getting what they want. Those things are: 1) lack of skill; 2) lack of courage; and 3) lack of resolve. As a band and individually, we've had to address each of these issues at one time or another. As a result, we've come up with strategies to address each. With these strategies, we've been able to access resources and answers that we didn't even know existed when we began. These strategies have helped us *Always Advance* towards our destination.

We call these strategies, "Cultivating the skill, the chill and the will."

The BrickHouse Philosophy says, "Cultivate the skill, the chill and the will."

Competence: The Skill

Skill simply refers to a baseline level of competence. In any vocation, you must have a certain amount of skill in order to succeed. You can't be a carpenter without a fundamental understanding of tools and how to build things. You can't be an engineer without an engineering degree and the credentials that go along with that profession. And you can't be a musician without some level of musical skill. You must have a baseline level of competence in order to succeed.

How much skill a person brings to a vocation varies. We can place skill into the category of a constant because how long you practice your craft or learn about your skill is entirely within your control. When I think of an extraordinary example of skill, I think of the former senator from New Jersey, Bill Bradley. Before he was a senator, Bradley had been an All-American basketball star at Princeton University and an Olympic gold medalist. Immediately upon leaving Princeton, he accepted a Rhodes Scholarship to Oxford University in England. When he returned from furthering his education, he joined the New York Knick NBA franchise where he eventually was part of two NBA championship teams.

Bradley was a great proponent of practice in order to cultivate skill. He realized he was not as big, strong or as fast as many of the opponents who played his position. As such, he practiced many hours in order to gain a variety of fundamental basketball skills. Even as a young boy, he imagined that when he wasn't practicing, there was someone out there who was. And when the two of them would meet, his opponent would win. Bradley understood the concept of competitive advantage even then. Like the boxer who gets up at 4:00 a.m. to run because he knows his opponent might be running as well, Bradley practiced in the gym long after everyone else had left. He practiced in the rain and snow. He cultivated an incredible work ethic that ultimately made him a world champion. He applied that same discipline to his academic studies. After practice, he was in the Princeton library studying until midnight. He set his sleep schedule at six hours and awoke every morning at 6:00 a.m. As a result, his education and training gave him the skills that enabled him to become a respected U.S. senator for eighteen years. In addition, he has also authored six outstanding books.

Following in that example, our BrickHouse Band drummer, Dale Drenner, still practices three hours a day. This is in addition to a full time job in the audio-visual field. When we travel, while the rest of us are sightseeing or otherwise engaged, Dale sits in his hotel room practicing riffs on his drum pad. Even though he is a master with incredible skills on percussion instruments, he is obsessed with improving. He has developed unparalleled speed, timing, and coordination through sheer daily effort. I have seen no one at any level in the Northwest with his skill set. He was not born with this; he has worked extremely hard and his work has paid off.

Skill simply boils down to education and practice. The education gives you the understanding. The practice gives you the skill. If you need to develop a skill to reach your destination, you need to arrange for the education. This could mean anything from getting a mentor to acquiring formal college training. It could require something as simple as reading a book or as complex as years of schooling at a variety of institutions.

The bottom line is... you need to develop a strategy and plan to acquire the skill necessary to reach your destination. You can use the same D-S-M-F formula that you learned in chapter two. Your education is an important interim destination on the road to your ultimate destination. And education should be ongoing. How long you practice what you learn is entirely your choice. Who knows, your practice might just overcome any talent deficiency you might have – and that could make the difference between success and failure.

The BrickHouse Philosophy says, "A baseline of competence is necessary, but winning is rarely about talent."

Hopefully, you have developed skills in an area where you have natural ability and talent. That falls in line with playing to your strengths. But you don't have to be the most talented in your field to successfully compete. Talent is a huge advantage, but winning is rarely about who has the most talent. Sometimes you might have another strength that can compensate for a particular lack of talent. Enter Henry Rollins.

Henry Rollins is a human dynamo. He never cared that he couldn't sing. He simply had a tremendous desire to perform and communicate. Even without a great singing voice, he recognized that he could deliver a passionate performance. All of this eventually translated itself into a one man entertainment industry. He began by fronting the punk band Black Flag in the 1981 before beginning the Rollins Band in the late 80's.

Essentially, Henry's singing boils down to rhythmic shouting that actually works for the type of music his bands play. His story began when as an 18 year old with a high school education, he was working in a Washington, D.C. ice cream store. He was a huge fan of the band, Black Flag. One night after work, he and a friend went to hear them perform. As a fan, he knew the lyrics to all of their songs. That night, as he stood in front of the stage mouthing the words to all the songs, they asked him if he wanted to come up and sing. Shocked, but recognizing the opportunity, Henry stunned everyone in the band with the intensity of his delivery. Because their lead singer wanted to devote himself to playing guitar, the band called Henry for an audition the following week. Henry showed up big time. The rest is history.

In parallel to his band work, Henry began to write. Again, as he would admit, the writing was not terrific. However, he kept at it. He was a voracious reader and like many writers, he learned about writing from simply reading. His writing skills improved. Soon, he was self-publishing books. He would sell them at spoken word concerts that he had begun to do when the band was on a break from performing. At these spoken word events, Henry would get up and tell stories. While not an amazing singer, he *was* an amazing speaker and story-teller, almost from the beginning. *This was the strength he could play to.* His audiences grew and he began to sell tapes and CDs of his spoken word performances. After a few years, he won a Grammy for one of his spoken word CDs. He appeared on The Comedy Channel. He served as host of a few different cable television shows. He got parts in several hit movies. He became a one man entertainment industry and still writes and sells out his spoken word concerts around the world at the age of 48.

Henry developed a baseline of skill in several areas. But his success was not simply about skill, and it certainly wasn't about talent. His success was primarily due to the qualities of desire and determination. He wanted it badly. He embodied the ideal of *Always Advance* as he continually learned, practiced and pushed forward. He relentlessly worked to develop himself, all the while putting products in the marketplace regardless of how they were viewed. He also had an incredibly thick skin to endure the criticism and ridicule he took for putting himself out there. He showed tremendous courage from the beginning as he continued to grow in skill. The BrickHouse philosophy has a name for this courage. We call it...*the chill*.

The BrickHouse Philosophy says, "Defeat the fear of death, and welcome the death of fear."

Courage: The Chill

Let's say that you now have a baseline level of competence and the necessary skill. But you still aren't advancing towards your destination. What's holding you back? What's keeping you from beginning anything that you want to accomplish?

Most likely, it's a lack of courage. To practice the *Always Advance* methodology, you will eventually have to demonstrate courage. First of all, please recognize that there is no shame in feeling afraid. Everyone feels afraid sometimes. After all, fear is the most pervasive marketing tool in the world. Why? Because it works. Just like negative campaigning is effectively used in political elections, fear is sold to consumers at every turn. But it's rarely blatant; it's often subtle. Because we are afraid of not being cool, we are inundated with messages about what car to drive, what deodorant to use, what computer to buy and what clothes to wear. If we don't purchase those products, we are told that we're somehow lacking as human beings. We'll be unlovable. This is of course, ridiculous, but sadly, it often works.

If you find yourself purchasing something because you believe other people will think more highly of you, you've been manipulated through the use of fear. If that doesn't bother you, fine. If it does, simply resolve to set your own standards for what you want to buy. Don't let an advertising agency decide for you. Recognize those advertising and media influences for what they are – and then make your own decisions as to what you want to purchase and how you live your life. That's one of the easier ways to practice and demonstrate courage. Recognize and resist manipulation.

Some people wonder why courage is even important

to address. Their lives are moving along just fine. They get up, perhaps they go to work; they come home, eat, feed the cat, watch some television and call it a night.

If you are one of those people and that's working for you – terrific! Seriously...enjoy. But I suspect that if you're reading this book, you're looking for something more. The life lived vicariously through others is probably growing weary for you. That's why the BrickHouse philosophy addresses courage because without it, we can't even begin to participate in our own lives.

We have literally become a nation of spectators. Why? In part because it is so much easier to watch other people put themselves at risk. We'd rather stay home and watch The Biggest Loser than go to the gym ourselves. We would rather watch other people compete to win a record contract. We would rather be idly entertained watching American Idol than actively engaged in our own creative pursuits.

Are we really that uninspired? Have we really lost our will to perform or produce something ourselves? Or are we simply afraid of how we'll feel about ourselves if we try something and do not succeed.

There have been numerous studies showing that people are happiest when they are engaged in some activity. They are happiest when they have lost themselves in something that challenges them to achieve something just beyond their reach, but not completely out of reach. *This requires the desire to participate! This requires that you select a destination!* And that will require courage.

Perhaps more than anything, we are held back because we fear looking foolish. This applies to just about everyone. For years Brooke helped people overcome their fear of public speaking by suggesting they sing karaoke. Recognizing that just getting up in front of people could be extremely intimidating; Brooke would sing along with them and help them feel comfortable. Brooke watched many people become more at ease performing and speaking through the simple practice of doing it.

Brooke knew this from her own experience. As a child, Brooke was painfully shy. But you would never believe that if you knew her today. In the following paragraphs, she tells the story of how she went from an introverted, reclusive bookworm – to the dynamic performer she is today.

> *I was always extremely shy and a typical bookworm. I would read and study for hours before practicing and studying classical piano and oboe. What very few knew is that at night the windows on the three walls of our large living room effectively became mirrors after the sun went down. When the lights went on inside the room, the walls became reflective. I danced for hours in this makeshift dance studio, practicing the moves I'd see on, "American Bandstand" and "Where the Action Is," as well as all those Beach Blanket Bingo-type movies. Back then I was comfortable around a friend or two, but in a group I became extremely self-conscious and quiet. My stage fright was overwhelming. Although I came from a musical family, I just couldn't perform by myself in front of people. Orchestra, band and choir were okay, but we soon discovered I absolutely froze on solos. Singing in front of anyone was the toughest – I could barely squeak out a tone even if only one oth-*

er person was within earshot. Speaking in front of the class was a terrifying blur – it was hard to breathe and I always ended my presentations with very little memory of the event.

I started "trying on" other personalities to get through group social situations. The character played by Marlo Thomas in the popular TV sitcom "That Girl" was a favorite of mine. She was bubbly, vivacious, and likeable. It worked. At the junior high graduation dance (a strictly no-dates-allowed social), I was surrounded by other girls who were nervous but just wanted to giggle and dance and have fun too. They were happy to have me (or Marlo) lead the way. (The crowning moment came when one of the girls, who I'd barely known before that evening, came up and said "You remind me so much of Marlo Thomas!" I smiled smugly. I had succeeded.)

So if I could be someone else, and I loved to dance, musical theater seemed like a natural. My mother drove my sister Sue and me to audition for the musical, "Oliver" at the local community theater. We cut our hair, put on boys' clothes and danced and sang merrily in the production. It was great – I had no fear in a chorus.

Then high school – I tried out for the part of Anne Frank's sister. I guess it went well – the director took me aside and said she'd like to consider me for the leading role. Oh, no – THAT was different! I refused, and landed the role of the sister, with very few lines, just as I wanted. Opening night, I was terrified. My legs would barely move, feeling like two 100 pound logs that I was force-

fully willing across the floor. One thing I was certain of – I would never, never, NEVER do another play!

So, obviously by the end of the run, I was over that. I loved acting – when I was on stage I wasn't shy me. I was whoever the script said I was, and that was easy. I landed and enjoyed numerous leads during the next eight years.

Extemporaneous speaking was another matter. That was me being me, and I was still very self-conscious and tongue-tied. Music was also too personal, too easy to be judged whether good or bad – I just couldn't solo, which we discovered as I continued to choke during either instrumental or vocal solos. Ten years later, I attacked that fear. Remember, I had already faced a similar terror once. I got over it by just doing it over and over until the fear subsided. So, by now I was a mortgage loan officer and the best way to get new clients was to have real estate agents forward their buyers. The way to reach agents, who are too busy selling to sit down and listen, was to bring donuts and speak at their morning meeting. My first presentation was set up by a good friend and I have to say, it was just awful. I was so nervous; I couldn't remember anything about anything. The office owner took pity on me and actually started feeding me questions with implied answers so I couldn't miss. I was a wreck, I hated the whole experience, but I was 26 and it was time to get over this fear. I set up more meetings, got better and better, and my nervousness subsided over the weeks. I reached the milestone where I was finally, actually over my fear of public speaking, simply by doing it over and over.

This confidence did not, however, carry over to musical performance. I was still far too shy to sing in front of anyone. So, another ten years rolled by. I had two daughters. The oldest was impossible to keep off anything remotely resembling a stage by the age of three. By the time she turned seven, she and her little sis were two of 8 children who toured the summer fairs and festivals, putting on a fairly high-level, choreographed musical show. Two of the others were my sister Sue's children, who were 9 and 12. During the five years the groups stayed together, we watched them perform in front of hundreds, and a couple of times thousands of people.

One night, my sisters and I were having a rare family get together at a restaurant that featured karaoke. Sue got up and sang, which was a surprise to me, and I asked her how she could possibly do that! She said, if our little kids could do it, we certainly could, too.

Wow.

I never thought of it that way, but she was right. About that time I talked to a classmate from twenty years before, who played drums and sang in a band, though he'd never shown any musical inclination in high school. He told me, he didn't start out being a singer but, "If you do anything enough times, you're going to get good at it. You just will." Oh. Alrighty then…

I located all the nearby karaoke bars. I went out three times a week, shaking with fear each time. Again, my first attempts were absolutely awful. Apparently when I got nervous my voice would simply go higher and higher. So there I am singing a Taylor Dayne song – I think it was "Don't Rush Me." The woman has a great range, but always spends part of the song in her rich alto voice. I was in terror, and I certainly had no alto voice that night. I ended up cracking jokes during the verses, just waiting for the chorus which went up into the higher registers. Jeez. It was not good. Terrified but determined although I was having no fun at all, I went up song after song, night after night, doing duets whenever I could because then I wasn't out there by myself. By the end of the night I was always more relaxed, but it was never easy. Then the owner of a karaoke company asked if I would like to be a karaoke host for his company. Mind you, I still had bad stage fright, but I had shown an ability to interact with the audience, so I think he forgot my voice wavered and cracked at the beginning of the evening. I accepted and decided to give it my best shot.

One of the places he put me into had just lost a much-loved host who had gone off to Nashville to try her luck at being a professional solo artist. I will never be in her league vocally, and as frightened as I was, well, you can guess at how well that went. The restaurant owner wanted me replaced, but the karaoke equipment owner convinced him to give me some time to settle in, and – curiously, as I sang night after night, and started working with others to get over their fears, my confidence grew and the trembling, even at the beginning of the night, faded away. A new clientele started coming in re-

peatedly – all those that were also too shy and needed someone at their elbow gently guiding them through the song, or having them sing from their chair for starters, until the shaking went away. To get over this fear, I just did it, and so did they.

One night shortly after Lee and I were married, a friend called me to tell me about her band. She was playing at a private club and wondered if Lee and I would come. She also asked if I would come up and sing backup on two old Motown songs. She needed one more singer to perform backup along with the wife of one of the band members.

I was very hesitant; I mean, I'd never sung with a band before. But while I was on the phone, Lee was nearby and he could tell what was happening. He vigorously nodded yes. He saw opportunity where I saw fear. But deep down, I knew I wanted to try it.

Once again, I had to go through all of the nervousness. But I pushed through it and the performance went well. Surprisingly, they asked me if I wanted to join the band as a permanent backup singer. This whole thing was getting out of hand. But Lee kept encouraging me and I joined. It was a great opportunity and it really helped launch the momentum and confidence that I needed when we decided to form BrickHouse.

I still get butterflies, and I can't say the terror doesn't briefly slip back when stepping out on stage after a long break from performing, but I just do it, and the fear always dissipates. I don't actually think about what my life would be like if I hadn't pushed through all the fear of stepping completely out of my comfort zone, but my life wouldn't be nearly as fun living with all those fears. I know that.

As Brooke's story indicates, doing the thing you fear is the fastest way to overcoming it – even if it doesn't happen overnight. Like Brooke, you can expand your comfort zone. You can increase the number of uncomfortable things you're willing to attempt. Whether it is speaking in public, skydiving or making that phone call to ask someone for a business loan, you can make the decision that life is too short to miss out. If you make a list of ten things you want to do, you might be amazed at how many of those things are actually available to you. Some of them could happen with one phone call! Others might take a few years of work. But whatever it is you want to do, don't let lack of courage keep you from it. Growth requires change and change only occurs when you move beyond the previous limits of your comfort zone.

But yes, doing it is easier said than done. How do you move beyond your fear to get to your interim and ultimate destinations? After all, it's easy to say *just do it.* But what kind of thought and physical processes can you put into practice to *just do it.* How can you practice being courageous?

The *Always Advance* methodology actually proposes a way of practicing "the chill." *The Chill Drill* is an eight step process you can use to develop courage. Yes, courage is a skill that can be learned!

I'll use an example that is occurring with me right this second. We'll go through it together and see how it works in real time. The value of *The Chill Drill* lies in the fact that it allows us to move through fear towards the destinations we have established in any area of our lives. It's simply another method that allows us to *Always Advance*.

Earlier, I mentioned our phenomenal BrickHouse Band drummer, Dale Drenner. Just one hour ago, I got word that Dale will have to have heart surgery to fix a leaky valve in his heart. It's possible that it could be open heart surgery. In the past hour, my stomach has cultivated that nervous feeling often referred to as butterflies. My palms are sweating and when I first got the news, my thoughts were racing in practically a panic attack. *And I'm not even the one having the surgery!* How must poor Dale feel?

Step one in *The Chill Drill* is to recognize the feeling of fear. The physical symptoms I just described have put me in touch with that. I definitely feel it right now.

After recognizing the feeling, ***step two*** is to simply STOP! Just stop and ask, "Am I okay right now?" My answer to that question is, "Yes." I'm experiencing the symptoms of fear but I am in no immediate danger. In this present moment, I am okay.

Step three is to ask, "What am I telling myself that's contributing to this fear?" Well, I'm telling myself that I'm afraid for Dale, not because I don't think he'll ultimately come through this okay, but because I know how much his health means to him. It allows him to play drums with reckless abandon and I know that certain kinds of surgery can take a tremendous physical toll on a person. It could mean a very long recovery time. Brooke and I love Dale deeply and we want desperately for him to be able to fulfill his purpose on earth. For him, it's to play drums. Our affection and devotion to Dale is limitless. So I fear for his well-being.

But that's just the beginning. I'm also afraid for the band. And selfishly, I'm afraid for me and what's going to happen. I'm afraid for the future of our entire enterprise. Dale has been with us longer than any other band member and he is the soul of our team. There are a thousand little things that he does to keep us all on cue. He is the piece of the puzzle that brings everything together.

Yes, we have very capable backup. That comes with being prepared. But will our backup be available? We have a summer full of shows coming up in one month and we're at a critical time in our growth. In addition, we're playing some amazing venues that I want Dale to experience. I hear myself saying, "Oh God, this is just awful. What if he has to take an extended time off? What if we go up to one of these pivotal shows we have and he can't be with us? What if we screw everything up? He's the glue! We're doing some intricate top 40 songs with difficult rhythms. We haven't got time to train our backup on the new songs. We've advertised those songs. We've billed ourselves as the type of band that can play these songs. What if we can't do the music we've promised? What's going to happen to us? What's going to happen to me and my dream of taking this band to an even greater level of success?"

Step four is to ask, "What are the facts?" Well, I know that Dale has to have surgery to fix a leaky valve in his heart. I guess I don't know for a fact if it's open-heart surgery. That's an assumption so I'll have to wait to find that out.

Step five is to ask, "Are my thoughts and feelings in line with the facts?" The answer is, "No, they're not." I don't know the details of the surgery and I don't even know if it's even scheduled. The details could be awful but I don't know that right now. Dale might be just fine. And I don't know how long Dale would have to be gone, if at all.

Another fact is simply that at this point, my thoughts have begun to take off on me. I've begun to think of this whole situation as a catastrophe. The fact is; I don't actually know how much danger Dale is in. I also don't know if the band and our dreams are in peril. In reality, this whole thing might just end up being an inconvenience; both for Dale and for us. I just don't know.

In addition, I also recognize that my ruminating on all of the horrible things that could possibly happen is not the best use of my present moment. It helps no one and it solves nothing.

Step six is to ask, "What useful action can I take right now?" First, I can regulate my physical body. I can breathe deeply. I can adopt a strong posture whether sitting or standing. Those are things I can immediately control and they help counteract the feelings of nervousness and fear. Next, I can send a note to Dale offering any and all assistance. I can tell him that we'll be here for him. Finally, I can begin using this moment to put together a contingency plan in case Dale is out for an extended period of time. I have a responsibility to the entire group to still be in the phone book when he returns. But again, I don't know how long he will be out, if at all.

Step seven involves asking, "What do I need to do in future moments?" In this case, I need to gather more facts as they become available – and remain steadfast in my support of my friend Dale and our team.

Step eight is to take action. Perform the necessary action from steps six and seven. Taking action is the best antidote to fear. And it is the only way to demonstrate courage. In this case, as I look at steps six and seven, I will:

1. Regulate my physiology by breathing deeply and adopting a strong posture.
2. Send a note to Dale offering all love and support.
3. Jot down a contingency plan to handle all upcoming shows.
4. Look up "leaky valve heart surgery" on the internet to learn more about it and remain conscious of following up on the facts as they come in.

As you move through this process, notice that steps two through five involve regulating and disciplining your thought process. It's not unusual for a person's thinking to run rampant and imagine every possible worst case scenario. After all, that's all fear really is; a thought process. If you disagree, I challenge you to take a shopping bag and go to the local mall. Fill your shopping bag with fear and bring it home.

Obviously, you can't. Fear is not a tangible object you can put your hands on. It's entirely based on perception and thought. It's simply a state of mind. That's why one person can be terrified of bungee jumping while another finds it to be a great time. It's all about each person's perception of the event and what he's telling himself about it. That's why steps two through five are designed to examine what you are telling yourself about whatever is making you afraid.

Steps two through five are also designed to bring you back into reality and to concentrate on the facts as you know them. This allows you to begin dealing with the things that are within your control.

So much of being afraid revolves around running worst-case scenarios in our heads. We project what we think we know into the future. We then convince ourselves that it is reality. As a result, anxiety, dread and panic begin to take hold. By "stopping" and disciplining ourselves to go through this process, we bring ourselves back from the future and into the present moment. After all, the present moment is where everything takes place. It's the only time in which we can actually do anything. And as you discipline your thinking, you can recognize that you don't actually know what's going to happen. So why be afraid of the unknown? After all, it's unknown!

Once you have your thought processes under control, steps six through eight concentrate on maximizing your physical body, making appropriate decisions, and acting on those decisions. The physical body is important because sometimes just taking on the physiology of courage helps bring it about. As performers, our band members understand this. They have years of experience performing in almost every imaginable circumstance.

Right before a performance, I watch band members as they begin to elevate their physical carriage. Their posture is lifted, they breathe more deeply and I can see them take on the characteristics of what is often called, "the matador's walk." A famous Spanish matador used to teach aspiring bullfighters to adopt the proud matador's carriage. His contention was that the carriage actually activated the necessary courage. Walking in an erect posture with head held high, he taught his students that "carriage preceded courage." Just acting the part of a courageous matador was sometimes enough to provide the emotional strength necessary to concentrate on the task at hand.

I remember watching our BrickHouse Band bass player, Greg Backstrom, walk into a venue before a show one New Year's Eve. He had his cool shades on and strolled in as if he didn't have a care in the world. Not cocky, just confident. There was no hurry to it, yet he projected a controlled energy that made me glad he was on my team. In reality, by day, Greg is a CPA and the Chief Financial Officer for several automotive dealerships. He understands being in charge. He probably handles more stress in a day than many of us handle in a month. But you'd never know it. He truly understands the relationship between carriage and confidence. His physical attitude is "cool executive" all the way to the bone.

In much the same way, our lead guitar player, Craig Coleman adds flashy, stylish dress to his physical attitude. It's a good thing because a cover band is only as good as its lead guitar player. Craig uses clothing in the same way that a matador might employ his cape. Craig knows he is good, and his clothes say it. In dressing the way that he does, he *has* to live up to the fact that he's out in front, bringing home the guitar solos that give style and flair to the band.

For myself, I am very conscious of getting into character before a show. To combat nerves, I breathe deeply and adopt a strong posture. If there's time, I then walk through the venue introducing myself to as many people as I can. I thank them for coming, ask them about what music they like and encourage them to enjoy themselves. If I have any personal doubts creep in, I have a mantra that I've used for several years. It is simply, *"I am the best there is."* This is not intended to be an arrogant or egotistical statement. Instead, it simply acknowledges my experience. It reassures me that for many years, I've had success in both music and public speaking. It reminds me that I can trust myself to come through just like I always have in the past. It gets me to a place of thinking, "Who better than me to be doing this? Who can I trust more than me?" The answer is always, "No one." When there is five seconds left in the game and someone needs to take the winning shot, *I want the ball*. Having reminded myself of this, I then take my attention off of myself, and put my energy onto how I can serve the customer.

As you get skilled in this methodology, you can begin to use what we call *The Modified Chill*. Under intense stress, when events are happening all around you, you may not have time to run through an eight-point checklist. In a very dynamic situation, you may only have time to ask, "What's actually happening" and "what do I need to do?" Then you need to act on your decision. In an emergency, you can run through *The Modified Chill* in a matter of seconds. It brings your attention into the now and forces you to decide on a course of action.

The Chill Drill

1. Recognize the panicked thoughts, the racing heart; the nervous stomach.

2. Am I okay right now in this moment?
3. What am I telling myself to feel this fear?
4. What are the facts?
5. Are my thoughts and feelings in line with the facts?
6. What useful action can I take right now?
7. What do I need to do in future moments?
8. Take action on what I need to do!

The Modified Chill

What's actually happening (facts)?
What do I need to do?
Act!

What if I'm Not Okay Right Now?

What if you're practicing *The Chill Drill* and your answer to number two is, "I'm not okay right now!" If you are bleeding or under attack, chances are that your instincts will kick in. If, however, you are frozen in fear, you still have to decide what to do and take action. In this instance, the definition of courage becomes the ability to think clearly under stress while continuing to advance towards your destination. If you are prepared for whatever emergency you're in, that will help. For myself, I've had performance situations on stage with the band where my technology has completely failed. In that circumstance, as my thoughts began to race, I had to continually bring myself back to my destination, or exactly what needed to be done right then and there. It helps to change any thoughts of "what's going to happen to me?" to "what do I need to do?" Committing sustained attention on what you need to do every moment keeps you locked in on doing the right thing. Concentrate only on what you need to do. Direct your attention to that one thing – and you'll be too busy doing it to notice that a few moments ago, you were feeling panic.

Perhaps one of the more notable examples of thinking clearly and acting courageously under extreme stress occurred on January 15th, 2009. On that day, U.S. Airways pilot Chesley Sullenberger was forced to land an Airbus 320 on New York's Hudson River. The airliner had collided with several birds causing both engines to fail. Not surprisingly, Sullenberger admitted that he was initially startled. But he and his first officer, immediately "moved on to the task at hand."

Sullenberger's only chance for success was to concentrate his attention on what needed to be done. By *moving on to the task at hand,* he had no time to think about being worried or afraid. He simply had to take action. Because he did, the lives of 155 people were spared.

How did he do it? Initially after the bird strike, he recognized that the engines had failed. Showing great self-awareness, he acknowledged that his physiological reaction to the situation was strong. He immediately forced himself to be calm. Within a minute of the engine failing, he realized he would not make it to any nearby airport. He then made the decision to land on the Hudson.

At that point, using great concentration, he thought of nothing but landing the aircraft. He knew what he needed to do. He recognized that when the airplane touched down on the water, the wings would have to be exactly level. The nose would have to be slightly up. In addition, he had to maintain a descent rate that was survivable. Amazingly, he was able to do all of those things.

It is worth noting that Sullenberger was probably more prepared for this situation than most. Just as we suggested in chapter two, *he had done his homework*. Prior to this amazing event, he had been an international speaker on airline safety. In addition, he had helped the airlines develop new protocols for safety and had devoted considerable time examining how the best cockpit crews handle crisis situations. Undoubtedly, he had already thought about how he would react under almost any type of airline emergency. But he also knew that no pilot in recent jet aviation history had ever negotiated a successful water landing. Airplane simulators don't even offer it as a training option. Yet Sullenberger's ability to recognize *what was actually happening* and *what he needed to do* provided a shining example for us all.

The philosophical title of this section is "Defeat the fear of death, and welcome the death of fear." This is a quote attributed to G. Gordon Liddy and its application for us rests upon the fact that we're all going to die. Most of us fear death. After all, isn't death the worst thing that can happen? While some might argue that point, we can at least accept death's inevitability. Once we accept that, we can stop fearing it. If you can find it within yourself to no longer fear death, every other fear that you can imagine begins to pale in comparison. It's quite liberating – and the experience of life becomes even more precious. In this way, death is a great teacher.

To the extent that you can eliminate fear from your life, you can create a freedom unlike anything you will ever experience. It's as if nothing has a hold on you any longer. It is perhaps the truest definition of independence. Just think of how you would feel if you no longer feared the disapproval of others and all that entails.

This lack of fear isn't a license to act recklessly or inappropriately. It is not license to shirk your responsibilities. I'm not suggesting that you think, "I'm no longer afraid of the consequences of not raising my children." NO! That's not what I'm suggesting.

I'm suggesting that it makes sense to recognize your obligations just as it makes sense to recognize real danger. But in recognizing real danger, you don't have to let it paralyze you; particularly now that you have a strategy that can lead you into acting courageously.

Imagine what might be possible for you to do if you were out from under the constraints of fear. Think of the confidence you could generate. Think of the energy you could manifest. Think of the amazing life you could be living.

The BrickHouse Philosophy says, "Be unreasonable, unrelenting, and unstoppable."

Resolute: The Will

Every life has defining moments. Businesses do as well. This particular moment applied to both. Two years after the night Brooke and I made the decision to form our band, we sat in our kitchen. We were nowhere close to stepping on that amazing stage that had initially launched our dream. Brooke was furious. Me? I was disgusted, disappointed and tired...very tired. We had struggled in those two years to build our band. We targeted clubs, casinos, parties and weddings anywhere in the Seattle area. With Herculean effort, we had continued to piece together a somewhat competitive group. We had made progress, but it always seemed like one step forward and two steps back. It was particularly challenging given that our daytime careers were extremely demanding. As a result, much of the work towards making the band successful occurred in the wee hours of the morning.

For the second weekend in a row, two of our musicians had not shown up for rehearsal. I was not feeling particularly forgiving and Brooke had completely had enough. We looked at each other. She read the weariness and disappointment on my face. At that time, we weren't good enough to be missing rehearsals. She picked up the phone and fired the bass player. She then called the lead guitarist and fired him as well.

I felt a certain relief, as if a giant boulder had been lifted from my shoulders. A huge part of me had wanted it all to be over. We had begun to play some decent venues but mostly, as is true when you're just starting out, you have to toil in some really bad places for very little money. You have to cut your teeth in biker bars, at street fairs and in places with stages the size of a postage stamp. Oh, I almost forgot, you're generally knee deep in somebody else's cheap beer while you're doing it.

The first actual show we ever did was an outdoor festival. We looked good but we were awful. Instead of the "The BrickHouse Band," the guy introducing us called us

"The Backstreet Band." I was glad. I didn't want them to remember us. In fact, Brooke was so mad at the drummer (this was before Dale joined us) that she stopped the show before we even did the last two songs. The second gig was at a small bar that didn't even have a stage. At this place, I had to physically escort a young man away from the band who was trying to get too friendly with our three women, who sing and dance out front. Because one of those ladies is Brooke, I'm a little touchy about overly friendly patrons.

It was just the worst. For two years, we played these kinds of gigs. Yet we wanted to succeed and we believed we had the formula for success. There was always just enough promise in all of it to keep moving forward. *And I wanted to win!* But I was beginning to have trouble justifying it all. The time and financial investments were substantial. So after Brooke finished firing the two musicians, I thought it was over. I had a million reasons running through my head for not continuing. Yet the idea of giving up disturbed me. Still, I knew that surrendering at that point would have been completely reasonable, logical and rational.

So I decided to test the waters to see where Brooke was at. In an offhand manner I said, "You know, we could bag this. We could go out to dinner like normal people on weekends; see a movie, meet friends. We could go on actual dates with each other and get home at midnight, instead of at 4:00 a.m. after shows."

Surprised, she looked at me as if I was from Mars.

She said, "I talked to a couple of guitarists the other day. They seem serious. Let's talk to them."

At that moment, I remembered again why I loved my wife. *She had just reminded me of who I was – a winner!*

In that instant, I changed. My back straightened. My jaw set. I was practically angry with determination. I was angry because I thought about all of the people who had predicted our failure – *and I had almost let them win*. I thought about how they said we didn't have the time, the money, or the chops to succeed. I thought about the people who said, "Oh, they're just going through a phase. Isn't that cute, they're starting a band." Even the ones that took us seriously said, "They're too old, too busy and they can't possibly succeed with all of the talent out there competing for the same jobs."

Finally, I thought about all of the people who said, *"They must be crazy!"*

I thought, *"YES! That's it! That's exactly right! We are crazy! You want crazy? I'll show you crazy! We are completely crazy and that's why WE will win!"*

Obviously, as I thought about the people who called us crazy, my demeanor was shifting. It shifted from a man who was beaten to a man who had absolute certainty that our project would succeed. It shifted from a man who was interested in being successful to a man who had *resolved* to be successful. Yes, we were completely out of our minds. Over time, that would ultimately prove to be the key to our success. Had we been within our right minds we would have done the sensible, logical thing – we would have given in. We would have quit. Who wouldn't? I'll tell you who wouldn't. We wouldn't! We wouldn't give up because yes, we were completely out of our minds. And once you get outside of your mind, you can look at it, examine it, control it – and most importantly, make it work for you.

We went back to work. Even when I had doubted,

Brooke had never lost sight of the destination. She always pictured us up on that big stage serving the public with an outstanding product. And just that little bit of encouragement, that little glimmer of enthusiasm from her was all that I needed to keep going.

I thought of George Bernard Shaw's statement, "The reasonable man adapts himself to the world; the unreasonable one persists in trying to adapt the world to himself. Therefore all progress depends on the unreasonable man."

I had always had an incredibly strong work ethic but now I was ridiculous. I redoubled my efforts. I made the decision that I would not be outworked. That's essentially all that is required; a simple decision. I decided that you might be smarter than me, more talented than me, better looking than me, and more popular than me – but you will not outwork me. Most of all, *you will not outlast me*! At the end of the day, I will make sure that my band is the "*last band standing*." Even if it is just me, a drumstick and a kazoo, I will not lose because I gave up and went home first.

Once again I recognized the value of the "Compete until you win" and *Always Advance*" attitudes. Can you will your mind and body to do things when they no longer want to? Can you handle the adverse conditions of fatigue, frustration and temporary failure? I decided that if our world became a battle of the bands, our competitors had better bring their "A game" and they had better bring it all day long if they were going to beat us.

Whether you know it or not, your business is in a *battle of the bands*. You're no doubt one band among many competing for the same market share. You must invoke an iron will that accepts nothing but success – and you must want to win badly.

Brooke and I now knew how badly we had to want this in order to succeed. We also recognized that our minds and bodies are much stronger and more capable than we often suppose. We had to be absolutely crazy in our desire to push through the fatigue, the disappointment, and the losses. But they're just losses, right? Again, big deal. So what! We decided that until we reached our destination, our band would not fall by the wayside for any other reason than we no longer drew breath. To do this, we would have to become unreasonable, unrelenting and unstoppable.

We would have to invoke the power of our wills and become *resolute*.

How it All Comes Together

If you have the skill, the chill and the will, you can make anything happen. Education and practice provide you with the necessary skill. Courage, or your capacity to chill, is an ability *that can be learned*. It will provide you with the momentum to implement your skill. Ultimately, courage amounts to thinking clearly, moving on to the task at hand and taking action on the thing that needs to be done. Finally, it is your ability to exercise your will and be resolute that will put you over the top. Genius is often simply resolve in disguise. Resolve to *Always Advance* until your destination is reached. Allow no excuse. Allow no one to outwork you. Allow no one to outsmart you. Above all, allow no one to outlast you. *Compete until you win.*

Key Points from Chapter Three

- There are only three things that keep people from ever getting what they want. Those things are: 1) lack of skill; 2) lack of courage; and 3) lack of resolve.
- In order to be competent you need skill. Skill simply boils down to education and practice. The education gives you the understanding. The practice gives you the skill.
- Winning is rarely about talent. Once you have a baseline of skill, it will be your own personal qualities that determine your outcome.
- Courage is a skill that can be learned. If you practice "the chill," you can expand your comfort zone and perform beyond what you thought was possible.
- Courage requires that you commit sustained attention on what you need to do while in the act of doing it.
- Resolve simply means to invoke your will and commit to the end. You must *Always Advance* through adversity and failure. If you experience a loss, simply get up and advance towards winning.
- Allow no excuses. Allow no one to outwork, outsmart or outlast you. Be unreasonable, unrelenting and unstoppable.

DALE DRENNER – Drums and Percussion

Courtesy of Lumina Photography

One of my favorite Dale Drenner stories occurred a few years ago. We were in a Seattle recording studio preparing to make a demo. The studio had recorded some big names like Carrie Underwood and we were excited to be there. The plan was to spend the first day laying down instrumental tracks. The second day we would record the vocals. The next two days would be spent mixing.

After Dale got his drum kit set up, he began to warm

up. I was in the next room. After a few minutes the studio head, who was also a touring musician, came up to me. Looking at Dale through a glass window he said, "Are the rest of you guys this good?"

I couldn't have said it any better. Dale is the very embodiment of the competence, courage and resolve that we highlight in this chapter. His amazing skill set is primarily due to the fact that he simply out-practices everyone else. Occasionally, we just send him out by himself to open a show. I just tell him to "Go out and get off. We'll be out in a minute." So Dale goes out and begins on the conga. The audience begins to get quiet as they begin to recognize that something extraordinary is happening. Dale leaves the conga and begins to work his way through the drum kit and after a minute, jaws are dropping all over the audience. It's one of the most fun things I get to do in the band; watch people's reactions to the fastest hands on the west coast. I love it.

Dale is very interesting to talk with because he's also a musical encyclopedia. He constantly listens to all kinds of music. I grabbed him for a few moments for the following Q & A.

Q: What unique quality or qualities do you believe have made you successful both in life and in the band?

A: Well, I really don't see myself as any different from anyone else. But I do love all kinds of music and I've always loved to play. I enjoy practicing and listening as much as performing. I think a commitment to practice and hard work are what make the best musicians stand out above the rest. I'm trying to instill those values in my kids as well. I also recognize that when I'm really focused, I can make everyone around me better. For example, if the band has a good night, but I don't feel I did, I think, "Well it's really not about me; it's about the whole package." If, on the other hand, the band had a bad night, but I thought I played well, I ask myself if there may have been something I did that caused the team to suffer. Did I really make a difference? Overall, it's the team that is important.

Q: What have you learned from your life experience that you've brought to the band?

A: I'm an army veteran and I really think that the discipline I gained in the service has translated well to my musical pursuits. Plus, in the service as in life, you have to work with a very diverse population. You have to learn to get along with all types of people and work as a unit – and certainly playing in bands involves all types of people as well.

Q: What have you learned from your band / music experience that you've taken back into your life?

A: I think the success I've had in music has given me confidence in other areas. Over the years, Lee and Brooke have counted on me to take more of a leadership role in the band. The success we've enjoyed has been extremely gratifying. Also, I'm a problem solver and in a band, sometimes you have to be analytical, dig in and just figure things out. I've taken that same problem solving mindset to my career in the audio-visual field.

Q: What do you value most about the other members of the band? What have you learned from them?

A: I've made some friends for life in this band. Plus, I really like that they aren't afraid to try new things. I've made several suggestions for songs to try and everyone has been open to hearing them. Many of them we've implemented. In turn, I've learned to listen to others' suggestions as well. I've learned that everyone has something to offer and if we capitalize on those strengths, we can do amazing things.

Q: What is your favorite band memory to this point? Any particularly humorous moment? Painful or embarrassing moment? Educational moment?

A: There are certain moments when things are clicking that sometimes stand out to me. Often, at the end of a three-set night, we'll each do a solo on the last song. A couple of weeks ago I was playing behind our bass player, Greg Backstrom, as he soloed. I was just giving him a little structure to riff off of. Greg starting doing a very common thing that jazz players do during solos... they use lines of music from other songs and take it out of the box. This night, for whatever reason, The Wizard of Oz music came out. We started with an up tempo jazz version of The Witch is Dead, which changed to an Afro-Cuban version of Somewhere Over the Rainbow. What was cool about that is how two people with different backgrounds can communicate on the fly. If we had planned to do that, it would never have worked.

Q: Do you have a particular philosophy of life that you embrace?

A: To me, work and play are the same thing. I have to enjoy both. If I'm not enjoying something, then I'm not doing it right, so why do it? That's why I hate vacations! I have to (but I don't) stop doing what I love and am supposed to do! But when I finally do relax, I read about music or the history of it.

BRICKHOUSE PHOTO SECTION

The girls strike a pose.

Courtesy of Amidst Vision Photography

Lee belts out a summertime jam.

Courtesy of Kristine Duncan

Costuming for All the Single Ladies!

Courtesy of Amidst Vision Photography

These are our little angels.

Courtesy of Lumina Photography

Greg workin' out a thumpin' bass groove.

Courtesy of Amidst Vision Photography

Brooke admires Lee's keyboard work
after he's admired her legs!

Courtesy of Amidst Vision Photography

Craig works the guitar in a funky festival shirt.

Courtesy of Kristine Duncan

Bumble bee black and yellow never looked this good!

Courtesy of Lumina Photography

Dale keeps everyone together with timing and skill.

Courtesy of Kristine Duncan

"Hey honey, every band has to play some of these smaller venues when they first begin!"

Courtesy of Kristine Duncan

Brooke, Kristi and Nikki are all energy!

Courtesy of Amidst Vision Photography

Attitude anyone?

Courtesy of Kristine Duncan

At the end of the day,
it's making people happy that counts.

Courtesy of Kristine Duncan

The BrickHouse Band in 2009

Courtesy of Lumina Photography

CHAPTER 4

Emotional Intelligence and Beyond: Your Personal and Professional Competitive Advantage

BrickHouse Principle Number 4: You must suspend your ego for the good of the enterprise.

So now you know where you're going. You've done your homework. You have the baseline level of skill and competence necessary to perform. You have the courage and resolve necessary to *Always Advance* and compete until you win.

There is yet one more factor that separates the rock stars of leadership and business from the ordinary rank and file...

That factor is called *emotional intelligence*.

The BrickHouse Philosophy says, "Without emotional intelligence, your skills, your talent and your I.Q. will not matter."

Daniel Goleman has been largely responsible for popularizing the concept of emotional intelligence within the United States. In addition to being a visiting Harvard lecturer, Dr. Goleman serves as co-chair of the Rutgers University-based Consortium for Research on Emotional Intelligence in Organizations. For the past fifteen years, his research has suggested that once people have certain baseline career competencies, it is their emotional intelligence that will enable them to rise above their peers. This has been particularly true for those in leadership positions.

My personal experience confirms this. After working in the aerospace business for twenty-three years and consulting with other businesses for the past several, I have seen this play out time and again. It's not that I.Q. isn't important – it is. But over and above I.Q., talent and skill, it is the emotional intelligence of both the leader and the collective team that accounts for whatever extraordinary successes occur. Conversely, a lack of emotional intelligence practically guarantees failure.

So just what is emotional intelligence? It's not simply one thing. It is the ability to understand your own emotional makeup. It also involves the capacity to stay aware of your emotions as they occur. It then involves using that awareness to make decisions that serve you and the common good. For example, if I've had a rough day at work, I might recognize that I'm feeling a little irritable. Given that, I'll use that awareness to avoid any potential contentious conversations when I get home. Perhaps I'll commit to staying a little quieter than usual because I know that when I'm cranky, I'm more likely to say something I'll regret. I recognize that it only takes one thoughtless remark to do irreparable damage to a relationship.

Who among us hasn't said something they'd like to take back. When you act with emotional intelligence, you rein in that desire to lash out. *You think things through*. You control your impulses before you speak and act. This ability to be cognitively aware is one of the things that separate humans from animals.

For example, both humans and animals are subject to a variety of stimuli. When confronted with a stimulus, they will respond. Graphically, a simple stimulus-response model might look like this:

Stimulus → **R**esponse

An animal receives a stimulus and responds accordingly. A human may do the same. However, a human has the ability to think before responding. This cognitive awareness creates a space for the consideration of any number of alternative responses. Thus, a human has the option of *momentarily stopping within that space to choose* a response.

Graphically, that might look like this:

S → **C**hoice → **R**

If your boss gives you a tongue-lashing, your first impulse might be to call him an idiot and tell him why he's wrong. However, you might be wise to stop and weigh your response. You might wish to say something that would be more helpful to your long-term best interests. This ability to stop gives you the power to *choose*. Because an emotionally intelligent person is self-aware, she will recognize and identify whatever emotion is stirred from this stimulus. If she is feeling anger, she can make the choice not to act on it. She has the power to choose a response that will help her in the long run. She can listen to her boss, weigh the feedback she's just heard, and rise above her anger to respond calmly in a way that helps everyone win.

What else characterizes emotionally intelligent people? People who are emotionally intelligent also understand what motivates them. They use that awareness to pursue goals that are meaningful to them. This gets back to our earlier question in chapter one of knowing "why" we're doing something. If you think you're doing something for money, you may later find out that the money doesn't satisfy you if you've had to compromise your values in order to get it. That's why it's vital to understand who you are and what you're about. Knowing "why" you are doing something allows you to make an emotionally intelligent decision before taking it on.

Emotionally intelligent people also have the ability to empathize. They can see things from the perspective of other people. Leaders who understand what others are feeling can take those feelings into account when making a decision that affects them.

This awareness of both self and others allows emotionally intelligent people to exercise social skills. It enables them to build relationships and develop social networks. With enough social skill, these people are able to influence others and promote their own personal or organizational agendas. In today's world, where social networking and a diverse global economy are increasingly relevant to our lives, social skills can mean the difference between success and failure.

I remember one instance early in our band experience when the lack of social skills was costly. We hired a very experienced and extremely talented female vocalist to join us. Brooke was excited to have her because she believed she would improve our sound and give us instant credibility within the Seattle cover band scene. In fact, Brooke had known her for some time and had long recognized her talent. Having met her on a few occasions, I loved her voice but had some reservations about her personality. Actually, I believe I used the words self-absorbed and egocentric to describe my initial reaction to her. And that had been my most conservative and kind assessment. Additionally, it concerned me that she never seemed to hang on very long with any particular band. But Brooke really believed in her so I put my reservations aside. I got on board and really rooted for her to succeed because *her* success would be *our* success!

Unfortunately, neither her success nor ours was to be a consideration. My initial assessment turned out to be correct. The only thing I could imagine worse than having this woman in my band would have been to be married to her. My three other male musicians at the time agreed. The word "diva" just didn't do her justice. Within four minutes of meeting the guys, she had alienated each of them. I am not making this up. She walked into our rehearsal room like a bull in a china shop. There was no *getting to know you* period. She just walked in, started giving orders and began to tell us how it was going to be. The guys looked at me in shock. I just shrugged and gave them a look that said, "Okay, calm down. Let's just give this a chance and see where it goes." The guys respected my wishes so they just gritted their teeth and sat back.

Before the end of her first rehearsal session, she had confronted my bass player and accused him of not being committed to the band. It didn't matter that he had forgotten more music than she'd ever known. It didn't matter that he had toured with Chaka Kahn in Europe and played with Klymax and George Clinton's Funkadelic, among others. She was quite certain that he was simply there to serve her needs. In reality, I was incredibly fortunate to have him in my troupe. I wasn't so sure about her.

I watched in amazement. Having lived through some forty-nine years of life at the time, I had never seen such a display of social ignorance. We had a gig coming up in ten days and Brooke talked me into keeping her to see if it could possibly work out. After all, she did have a terrific voice. At this point, it would have been difficult to find a replacement so I let it ride.

Before the show, her high-maintenance persona grew even worse. She would call me at inopportune times during the day and say, "We need to change the harmonies," or "you need to tell the guys to play quieter." As I spoke with her, I did my best to practice my own version of emotional intelligence by simply listening. Without committing to anything, I placated her and promised to think about what she said. Inside, however, I was boiling. I was most definitely aware of my emotions and I was regulating them as best I could.

The evening of the show finally came. It was at a medium-sized bar but I wouldn't call it up-scale. Actually, it was a dive. But when you first begin, you play the places that will hire you. Surprisingly, the first set went pretty well. I began to feel encouraged. However, unbeknownst to me, our little diva had brought her boyfriend along, a self-proclaimed sound expert. He was in fact, a musician with another band and probably did have some sound expertise. But like his girlfriend, he had very little in the way of social skills. He was talking and gesturing very loudly about how the sound wasn't right. He was causing a scene and definitely not adding value to our situation. He badly wanted attention. So instead of getting to spend time with patrons between the first and second sets, I had to spend my valuable time calming him down.

As we began the second set, I noticed that our little diva now had a drink with her on stage. Apparently, she had consumed some on the break as well. I had been too busy babysitting her boyfriend to notice. Let it be on the record that I don't allow our band to drink at shows. Ordinarily I have nothing against alcohol but we're paid employees and it's just not a good idea. If we're playing a private party and the host (read customer) insists we have a drink towards the end of the night, fine. But that's the only time; never in a club or at a corporate event.

The reasons why I have a no-drink policy became readily apparent that evening. I watched in half-fascination, half-horror as diva-girl leapt from the stage to the top of a huge square bass speaker that was on the floor in front of the stage. From there, she got into a baseball catcher's crouch and began bouncing up and down like a chimpanzee on crack. I'll never forget it. I could tell from the look on Brooke's face that even she was stunned.

After the second set, I walked out into the crowd. I really wanted the night to be over. A guitar player with another band was in the audience. He was someone whose opinion I respected. He stopped me and asked, "Hey Lee, where did you get the trailer trash?"

For me, his rhetorical question really summed up the situation quite nicely. As such, I did the only thing a man in my position could do. I tossed my wife under the bus. Abruptly, I answered, "Ask Brooke!"

I was fuming but could not let on. I had to rein in my emotions and continue to serve the customer while figuring out how to do damage control to our reputation. On the ride home from the show, Brooke didn't even give me a chance to say it. She said, "Don't worry, she's gone. We'll start interviewing this week."

I responded, "Could we please get someone who plays well with the other children?"

"Yes," Brooke said. "This time, social skills will come first, voice second."

"Maybe we could get both," I said.

"Hey, there's an idea!" Brooke laughed.

We filed that experience under lessons learned and moved on.

In a very real sense, emotional intelligence is indeed about playing nicely in the sandbox with the other kids. It involves maturity and awareness, both of self and others. In his original studies, Goleman identified what he called the five components of emotional intelligence.

1. Self-awareness
2. Self-regulation
3. Motivation
4. Social Awareness (Empathy)
5. Social Skill

These five components are the hallmarks of an emotionally intelligent person. If you are not self-aware, if you can't handle your own emotional distress, if you are not motivated to achieve, if you do not understand the concerns of others and do not manage relationships successfully, it won't matter how bright or talented you are; your life will be a struggle.

Whether you are talking about working within a company, a band, or just managing a relationship, being skilled in these five components can help you navigate through all kinds of difficult situations and problems.

Within these five components, I've identified eight characteristics that if practiced successfully, can elevate anyone to the top of their profession.

1. Perspective – See the bigger picture. Putting things into proper perspective gives an appropriate sense of proportion to life events. Most things are not "life and death." Don't treat them that way.
2. Initiative – Take the lead. Be first. Go get what you want.
3. Insight – Take an objective look at your situation. See it clearly and take responsibility for your contribution to any problem you might be facing.

4. Solution-orientation – Identify the problem but don't dwell on it. Move immediately into finding a solution.
5. Willingness to risk – Try something new and you may experience tremendous growth – but be conscious of not doing harm.
6. Delay gratification – Be able to put off an immediate reward for a greater long-term payoff.
7. Resourcefulness – Use whatever is at your disposal to succeed.
8. Perseverance – Keep going, particularly after others have given up.

One of the great joys about leading the BrickHouse Band has been watching the growth of our collective emotional intelligence. Having had several shared performance experiences, each of our members knows what it feels like to be in the others' shoes. That gives us an empathic sensitivity that manifests itself whenever we collectively critique our performance. There is an understanding among us that when feedback is given, it's not criticism per se. It's simply an attempt to make our performance better as a whole. No one lashes out and yells, "You didn't play that right!" Our approach to criticism is usually couched in the form of a question. For example, someone might begin a critique like this: "I'm wondering if those are the actual notes we are supposed to play there. Maybe we could listen to the original just to make sure we're hitting this correctly."

There are no accusations in those statements. There is no finger pointing. There is no competing with one another to see who is better. There is no drama. Those statements lead to productive dialogue that focuses on how we can improve.

While giving feedback in this way should be a no-brainer, believe me, it's not. I've been in any number of musical and/or business situations where people lashed out in an accusatory fashion. This lack of respect for others shows a fundamental deficiency in emotional intelligence. Unless it can be fixed with education, it will ultimately be the death knell for your band or your organization.

The good news is that you *can* fix this with education. It's not always easy and it's not always rapid – but emotional intelligence can be learned. We've had success within the band by remaining mindful of the following points:

- If someone makes as mistake, don't criticize and condemn...coach and educate.
- If everyone disagrees, to the extent possible...mediate towards a solution.
- If someone suggests an idea...listen and honor the idea, even if it can't immediately be implemented.
- If there is confrontation, instead of fighting... negotiate.
- If bad news comes, don't run from it. Deal with it right away.

Implementing these ideas can help your team immediately become more productive.

Emotional intelligence boils down to your ability to recognize, understand, manage and use your emotions. Knowing that emotional intelligence dramatically increases your probability for success, what is the most efficient and effective way to begin learning to improve it? You can most improve it by working to enhance the one common denominator that runs throughout the entire discipline… *awareness*. Awareness is the one quality above all others that truly characterizes an emotionally intelligent person.

When you are more aware, you see more clearly. When you see more clearly, you understand more fully. When you understand more fully, you make better decisions. It's really that simple.

But how do people improve their ability to become aware? After all, you have to *be* aware in order to know if you actually *are* aware!

That's a fair point. But if I told you that there was one thing that could help you become more aware, would you do it?

You may not like the answer, but here it is.

The BrickHouse Philosophy says, "To find the groove, you've got to get out of your own way."

The answer to developing increased awareness can be found through meditation. It need not be a formal meditation practice, although if you were to study under a skilled teacher, you could help yourself considerably. However, if you don't want to go to that extreme, I would recommend a simple *mindfulness meditation* practice.

Mindfulness meditation is a wonderful way of increasing awareness because you are simply sitting and observing. Your task is to just pay attention to the moment you're in. Whether paying attention to your breath, a phrase or a mantra, you simply sit and breathe and pay attention. That's all; nothing more.

I recognize that most of our population would consider sitting, breathing and paying attention as something akin to torture. Just sitting still, let alone not accomplishing anything, probably seems like a complete contradiction to a methodology proposing that you *Always Advance*. Believe me, it's not. Stopping to observe and gain control of your mind is one of the most productive things you could ever do. It allows you to slow down and take stock of where you're going. And you already know that you can't advance if you don't know where you're going.

Practicing mindfulness meditation costs nothing. But it does require that you stop. It took me a very long time to learn to sit still for five minutes. But over time, I learned to be comfortable for much longer periods. My practice now consists of 15 to 20 minutes of sitting, five days a week minimum. Thirty minutes to an hour would be even better; however, that much time would be a luxury for most people.

In today's society, we all feel the pressure to be accessible. If the blackberry isn't within reach, we start to believe we'll miss an important call or a potential client. Or we believe every second has to be filled with activity. Perhaps. But in reality, stopping for twenty minutes to gain control of ourselves and our mind is incredibly productive on a practical level.

When you have control of your mind, you can place it on what needs to be done. You can deliberately set out to accomplish your aims. Mindfulness meditation will help you gain control of yourself – and control of yourself is the hallmark of an emotionally intelligent person. You are not just randomly doing whatever task you find is in front of you. You are acting upon the world with your own agenda. The world is not acting upon you.

How do you begin practicing mindfulness meditation? It's simple. You sit and concentrate on your breath. If your mind wanders, you just observe your thoughts without judging them. You might think *isn't that interesting* and then bring yourself back to your breath until the next time your mind wanders. Once again, just catch yourself observing those thoughts and bring yourself back to the present.

What you begin to notice is how "all over the map" your thoughts are. Sometimes you think crazy things and other times you think about the fact that you're hungry, or that you forgot to bring home that report from work. It's completely normal to have these thoughts and it helps to think of them as just clouds passing overhead. You just watch them without judging and let them go. Then bring yourself back to your breath.

In the simple act of observing your thoughts, you increase your self-awareness. You also begin to understand that you don't have to identify with your thoughts. You are not your thoughts. If you were, who is it that's watching and observing them? You are the observer. The thoughts are what are being observed. As such, you realize that *the real you* can change your thoughts, or send them away completely. You can take control of your mind if you choose to.

We've included simple instructions for a mindfulness meditation practice in Appendix III. This practice of observing your mind is what facilitates an increased awareness in your day-to-day life. This awareness enhances your emotional intelligence. In stopping to observe your thinking, you open the door to new options that can lead to better outcomes. You slow yourself down and connect to the moment you are actually in. You create a space to hold your thoughts and examine them. Within that space, it's as if you have created your own cup of awareness that contains your thoughts.

You begin to carry this awareness into real time. For example, instead of being baited into an argument with a loved one, you find yourself observing your thinking. As an alternative to an old response like, "Why is it always my fault? Why are you always blaming me?" You might instead opt for a new response such as, "I can see why you are upset. How can we solve this?"

This real-time awareness is just one benefit that can accrue from a mindfulness meditation practice. In addition, the *dis-identification* with your thoughts allows you to assume a detached calm. After all, you're just watching and paying attention. As a result, you have the option to get out of your own way. You begin to notice when you find yourself over-thinking something. You recognize your tendency to over-analyze and sabotage your own success.

It is truly amazing when you realize that you can gain skills in handling your mind simply from sitting and observing it. This is to say nothing of the health benefits you may gain such as lower blood pressure and an increase in energy.

You may also be surprised to find that you gain insights into your personality. As you observe your thoughts over time, you begin to see their connection to your behavior. You begin to understand why you act the way that you do. The option to change becomes a very real possibility because you stop worrying about later on and how difficult it will be to change. Your awareness has connected you to the now – and right now is when everything occurs. As such, self-improvement can now be practiced in the present moment. You don't have to concern yourself with improvement later on. Later on doesn't exist. You can simply practice being your best self right now. When later on becomes now, if you remain aware, you'll still be practicing in the present moment. See? You're improving already!

In addition to meditation, there are other techniques that you can use to improve your emotional intelligence.

1. Some of the greatest advice ever given comes in grade school. I remember our first grade teacher telling us that before we cross the street, we should stop, look, and listen. She was trying to keep us safe from oncoming traffic. Yet this lesson applies to so much more. If we stop, look, and listen during the course of each day, we'll remain much more aware of our surroundings and what is really happening. In addition, we might just keep ourselves from acting in a self-sabotaging manner. Stopping momentarily before acting or speaking can pay huge dividends.
2. Make a list of your hot-buttons. If you know what sets you off, you can mentally rehearse how you will respond in advance.
3. Practice role-playing new responses in order to see how comfortable they are. Performing the actual behaviors before having to do them under stress will make them much easier to execute at crunch time.
4. Ask your loved ones to give you feedback when

they see you slipping back into inappropriate responses. Promise them that you will listen and not overreact. Then go to work on new responses.

5. Take time to really consider what motivates you. Be honest. Jot down whatever comes to mind. Don't worry if your motivating forces are largely driven by ego. Recognition, love, money, and fame are typical motivators for people. If the first thing you jot down isn't a desire to serve humanity, that probably just makes you honest. Don't worry about that for now. Just get in touch with the things that motivate you.

As you gain more awareness and insight into your behavior, you may also notice that in the past, you have felt the need to defend your conduct. You may have often felt the need to argue and prove yourself right. We've all been down these roads so I'm not going to suggest that you subscribe to a twelve-step program for recovering egomaniacs. However, a brief discourse on how suspending your ego can occasionally be useful is now in order.

The BrickHouse Philosophy says, "If you don't care who gets the credit, your team can reach any destination."

Personally, I don't think a healthy ego is a bad thing. That's probably not surprising from someone advocating an *Always Advance* performance methodology. Someone who competes to win is generally going to have an ego. Having said that, it's up to you to control and direct your ego. You can't let it control you. And you can only do that by being aware of it at all times. So what exactly do we mean by ego?

For our purposes, the ego is that part of you who sees itself as *special* and separate from everyone else. This only becomes a problem when it sabotages your team's arrival at your agreed-upon destination. Because a well-functioning team can usually achieve more than an individual, reaching your destination may mean that you have to put your *specialness* aside. That's why it's essential to be aware of when your ego wants to put yourself above the team.

If everyone on your team signed on to the vision and mission that said you were going to Seattle, but you suddenly decided to go to San Francisco, you are sabotaging your teammates. After all, you'll probably need to take some of their precious fuel that they need to get to Seattle. You may also need to grab the map and reroute the GPS system, thus confusing your teammates who have agreed to stick to the plan. In addition, someone else will have to pick up the slack for the work you're no longer performing.

But you're special, right? You're unique and gifted. Well, maybe you are. You may indeed be the best performer on your team. Maybe you're carrying more than your share of the load. Maybe you warrant greater monetary compensation for your service. Maybe all of those things are true. If so, there will be a time when those things will need to be addressed. *But not until you reach the destination you signed on for!*

If, in your *specialness*, you start doing your own thing, your teammates will have to regroup. They'll have to reroute their map in order to reach the destination that you agreed to help them reach. With or without you, they are still bound by their commitment. And if they are truly a well-functioning team, that's not just a problem for them. It's a problem for you as well because without realizing it, you are blowing your chance to be a winner.

If you are part of a team, play the role that you agreed to play and be quiet. In my opinion, that would be the emotionally intelligent thing to do. Why would anyone want to hear a word about how special you are until you've accomplished something. That means *reaching the destination*. When you get there, we'll talk. Seriously, we all want to be compensated according to our contributions. But if you are contributing to a cause that's not winning, why should I compensate you like a winner? If you're not reaching the destination, I can find someone for half the money who can also not reach it.

To illustrate, several years ago when Seattle still had a professional basketball franchise, they were suffering through a very mediocre season. They had many people frustrated because they were an immensely talented team. But they weren't performing anywhere near to their potential. Why? They had twelve massive egos with personal destinations that were more important to them than the team destination, which was to win a championship.

Several players on the team were screaming that they needed more playing time. Their personal statistics meant far more to them than whether the team won or lost. After all, they believed that they could use those statistics to negotiate their next fat contract. Every day in the newspapers there were stories of unhappy players whining and complaining. The coach had a real problem because in fact, most of the team was of equal ability. But you can only put five guys on the court at a time. And no matter who he played, they still kept losing!

As if this wasn't enough, all of these talented players were making huge salaries. The team management was upset because these salaries were pushing the limits of the salary cap under which, by rule, the team had to abide. Problem solver that I am, I had a solution. My solution would completely fix the salary cap issue and eliminate much of the whining about playing time.

I wrote to the Seattle Supersonics general manager and sent copies to the owner and head coach. I got a buddy from work to join me and we volunteered, at great personal sacrifice, to join the team for a mere $100,000 apiece. That way, the team could drop two players with huge salaries who were whining about not getting enough playing time. This would literally save them millions of dollars and my buddy and I would never say a word about playing time. Not a peep. We would happily sit on the end of the bench. In fact, we would *insist* we not play. After all, he was 5′ 6″ and I was 5′ 8″ – it wouldn't be pretty!

We envisioned calling ourselves "the salary cap guys." We'd write a screenplay based on our experiences and the movie would star Billy Crystal and Michael Keaton as us. Sadly, hard as it is to imagine, we never heard back from the team. They just continued to lose. They continued losing because the players could not suspend their egos long enough to put winning ahead of what they perceived to be their own personal gain.

And to think, my buddy and I could have helped them lose for a lot less money.

Sarcasm aside, there is a point to this story. Big egos

that don't participate for the good of the team will contribute to you being a loser. Businesses routinely throw money away on these big egos. Don't be one of them. Certainly, you could argue that professional basketball is entertainment and if they were entertaining, the players earned their money. Perhaps. But the destination they signed on for was a championship – and they came nowhere close. If your business is coming nowhere close to its best, you might take a look at your personnel, your salary structure, and most importantly – what gets rewarded.

This brings up a simple but profound truth. *What gets rewarded gets done*.

It's hard to blame the Seattle players in our story. After all, they were highly paid whether they won or lost. Other than perhaps a championship ring and some possible endorsement opportunities, the rewards for winning and losing were just about the same. So losing really didn't impact their bottom line. They believed that their personal statistics were more important to their compensation and they performed accordingly. In reality, they were probably correct. *Had they only been paid when they won games, you would have seen a massive behavior change*. Team play would have accelerated at warp speed. Unselfish behaviors that lent themselves to winning would have been the rule rather than the exception. They could have indeed won an NBA championship.

This is just as true in business. Organizations within the same company will sometimes pad their own statistics at the expense of another organization. They will do this even if it subverts the company's ability to win and succeed. Why? Because they get rewarded for that behavior. This sub-optimization is common and can be a real problem. If I'm a salesman and I'm making promises that our service department can't deliver, I'm helping my immediate bottom line but hurting the business. I'm also hurting my long term interests as well because I will lose the goodwill of my customer base.

In business, you have to create a culture where people understand that long-term interests and team victories are the only victories that matter. In a world where next quarter's profits are your measure of success and where people want to be individual stars, that's a tough sell. But you can see the results of not selling it. You get an *every man for himself* mentality. A few people win in this scenario, but the economic culture eventually collapses.

You can imagine the difficulties that come up in the music and entertainment business with an *every man for himself* mindset. There are some enormous egos in the music business and they want to be stroked. Plus, there is a tremendous amount of competition. In order to stand out, it's normal to think that you have to be a "star."

We solve that problem in The BrickHouse Band by ensuring that everyone has an opportunity to "star" during a show. We make sure that they get at least one and hopefully more opportunities to show their strengths and be recognized for them. But more importantly, we do it within the context of a team victory. We make sure that each person's starring moment makes our entire enterprise look good. As a band leader, I have to walk a fine line between making sure our team has fun, grows, and gets to do some of the things that they'd like to do artistically, while balancing that against what the customer wants. I have to be able to create a space where the band can thrive yet still serve the customer.

Now that we follow the *Always Advance* methodology, we only hire people who are intelligent enough to understand that our business is about the customer. Our band gets it. That's why we've survived in an unbelievably competitive market. The bottom line is that we have created a reward structure that is based upon our entire band reaching our destination. For us, it's a team victory that serves our customer or it's nothing.

I'm not saying that you shouldn't have personal goals. I'm simply saying that in order to win as a team, your personal goals have to fit within the framework of the team's goals. There will be times when you may need to sacrifice for one another. You may have to share the glory. As in baseball, you may be called upon to lay down a sacrifice bunt that moves the runner from first to second base. You'll make an out but the runner will advance. Sometimes we take one for the team. That might mean that just like in sports, we have to perform when we're hurt or not feeling well. That might mean that we give up a song that we'd really like to sing to a teammate. It might mean that we have to play a minor role for a while. But playing a minor role on a championship team still makes you a champion! Playing a major role on a losing team might mean you're great individually, but you'll never be remembered as a champion.

In 2009 alone, our seven band members have had three collective *major* surgeries. *No one missed a gig!* Close relatives have died. Business nightmares have occurred for many of us in our day jobs. We've had consecutive gigs on consecutive days on opposite sides of the state while people have had to work the next day. *They still show up for the team!*

Talk about team building! Talk about respect! Our unit shows up when they've just had stomach surgery, heart surgery, a finger cut off and major assorted traumatizing injuries. We're just a band but these are people I would go to war with any day! *These people compete to win and they do!*

It's taken many years but we finally have a band that understands that to be successful as a team, they must suspend their individual egos. Of course the beautiful irony of this is that each of them goes much farther individually because of it. Their willingness to be team players has made each of them a star. As such, they are still in the game while many other excellent musicians who haven't learned to control their egos are not performing. They never got the lesson. If you don't care who gets the credit, you'll get much farther much faster. In addition, I know that all of them have tapped into strength that they never knew was in them.

Perhaps most gratifying for Brooke and me is that we get to witness the joy that each of our band members feels when one of the others succeeds. You can truly accomplish anything when this kind of selflessness is at the core of your team.

The BrickHouse Philosophy says, "A generous and abundant spirit attracts the best of everything."

Of course, you have to be able to suspend your ego in order to exhibit this kind of selflessness. Once again, it requires being emotionally intelligent enough to be aware that your ego has taken over. I would challenge you to examine your own ego. You'll know that you've lost control whenever you begin to believe that the world is here to serve your needs, or that you deserve special treatment. You'll know that you've lost it when it becomes more important to be right than to listen to alternative arguments. Again, you may well be the best at what you do, but if you're constantly reminding everyone of that, they'll soon tire of hearing it and you'll be talking to yourself. Yes, you're special. But so is everyone else. Taking a little time to acknowledge the worth of others will go a long way towards helping you succeed as well.

The opposite of an out-of-control ego is a generous and abundant spirit. What does it mean to be abundant? For our purposes, it means to be amply supplied in resources with an unlimited ability to generate more. It's largely about being self-confident and secure within your own abilities. And if you have mastered the skill, the chill and the will, you already know that you are capable of generating whatever you need.

The belief that you can generate whatever you need lends itself to a generous spirit. Do you see the root of generous in the word generate? Your abundant attitude makes it easy to be generous with your own resources. If there is always enough, you can feel free to share because you will never lack. The resources you share may include time, money, information and material possessions. Whatever it is, you feel free to share because you know there will always be enough.

Having said that, this is not license to be abused or

taken advantage of. This is where the BrickHouse philosophy deviates from much of the "new age" literature that has been popular over the last two decades. Your generous and abundant spirit is going to attract many people. It will attract quality people and it will also attract those who would abuse your generosity for their own gain. Fortunately, it takes about thirty seconds to figure out one from the other. You can generously show those who would abuse you how they too can be abundant – and give of themselves. Once you've gotten to the part about giving of themselves, they'll disappear. Problem solved.

People with abundant spirits have no need to talk trash about their competitors. They spend no time envying or hating those who are excelling in their field. Instead, they work to emulate those who are successful. Not surprisingly, they often get help from those very people. After all, quality people tend to want to hang out with other quality people. Water seeks its own level. This generally leads to productive things happening. When productive activities are a part of your life, you find yourself feeling grateful. In fact, when you are generous with your abundance, you find that your life overflows with gratitude. You'll experience the gratitude of others and more importantly, you'll feel grateful for the abundance you have. When you practice gratitude, you get to participate in the ongoing experience of real joy. You experience real joy because you are living a life of love, not of lack.

You may wonder how we reconcile this abundant attitude with the philosophy of competing to win. Aren't those two ideas a contradiction? Not at all. When we're competing to win, we're challenging our competition to raise their game. If they do, the marketplace and consumers benefit. We believe our competition can do much better, as can we. Our goal isn't to put them out of business. Our goal is to force them to be the best they can be. Isn't that good for them? In turn, it's good for us because we have to *Always Advance* and continuously improve in order to stay ahead. So let's have some fun and see who can do the best job serving customers!

The practice of abundance and counting your blessings increases your personal well being. In addition, your attitude has a positive impact on your environment. Your team and everyone around you will benefit. If you can focus on what is right with your life as opposed to what is wrong, you will bring on a shift that will transform your entire existence. This attitude is entirely up to you. It is a choice.

The richest people on earth are the ones who appreciate what they have. No one who is grateful is unhappy. *Think of the amazing blessings that are yours every day.* Be grateful that you still have a heartbeat. You're still in the game! If you have forgotten the amazing abundance that you have, consider those that don't have enough food, shelter, or clothing. Even in times of recession, our quality of life is unparalleled in the history of the world.

If you wake up in the morning and you find yourself complaining, stop and ask yourself, "Is there really anything to complain about?" If you're going to work, you can be grateful to have gainful employment. Why complain about that? You have the opportunity to contribute at work and to reap the rewards.

If you're getting up and having breakfast, be grateful

for the food. Be grateful for the transportation that takes you to work. Be grateful for the family that you get to provide for – or whatever else motivates you to contribute.

Be grateful for the people you get to work with each day. Chances are they have become friends. If you want to make more friends, serve someone. Put out just a little extra energy. Be grateful for the energy you have that gives you the opportunity to serve others. Serving others and thanking them is the most wonderful way to express your gratitude. *Gratitude and service are two sides of the same coin*. Bringing appreciation, service and love is the most certain way to immediately experience unlimited abundance.

In addition, be grateful for the educational opportunities that are available to you. This includes the amazing literature that exists no further away than your library or internet connection.

Be grateful that you live in a country where you have the opportunity to choose.

Be grateful that you have freedom. You have the freedom to do what you love – and to love what you do. Best of all, you get to choose how you will use this spectacular freedom.

In closing, please remember that you will continue to attract more of what you want when you pay attention to what you have as opposed to what you lack. In addition, you begin to appreciate everything that happens to you. You begin to understand that everything that happens to you can be of some value.

You begin to grasp the theme of the next chapter: *leverage everything*.

Key Points from Chapter Four

- Emotional intelligence separates the rock stars of leadership and business from the ordinary rank and file.
- Emotional intelligence involves the capacity to stay aware of your own emotions and those of others. It then involves using that awareness to make decisions that serve you and the common good.
- The components of emotional intelligence are:
  - Self-awareness
  - Self-regulation
  - Motivation
  - Social Awareness (Empathy)
  - Social Skill
- Awareness is necessary in order to be proficient in emotional intelligence. This awareness can be effectively developed through mindfulness meditation.
- As a leader, remember that what gets rewarded is what will get done.
- In order for a team to reach a destination successfully, individuals on that team may need to suspend their own egos.
- The richest people on earth are the ones who appreciate what they have. No one who is grateful is unhappy.
- Gratitude and service are two sides of the same coin. Bringing appreciation, service and love is the most immediate way to experience unlimited abundance.

GREG BACKSTROM – Bass and Vocals

Courtesy of Lumina Photography

If you enjoy a high-powered intellect with a strong dose of humor tossed in, you'll love BrickHouse bassist Greg Backstrom. After touring as a professional musician for many years, one day Greg decided to use his education and get a "real" job. Now a licensed Certified Public Accountant, Greg serves as the Chief Financial Officer for several Northwest car dealerships. Those of us in the band prefer to think of his day gig as his part-time job. In reality, Greg routinely puts in ten to twelve hour days before coming out to play with the band. His stamina is legendary. But it is his amazing emotional intelligence that has earned him a place in this chapter.

The chemistry of the band immediately improved the day Greg walked in the door. His humor, his willingness to sacrifice himself for the team and his agreeable nature were just what the band needed. Of course, his excellent musicianship didn't hurt either. His skills with a bass guitar along with his quality vocals have captivated audiences up and down the west coast. But Greg is one of those incredibly bright individuals who know just what to say and when to say it.

Greg is a leader. It is no accident that he is successful in everything he attempts. As a musician, businessman, husband and father, Greg sets an example that anyone would do well to emulate. We are proud that he represents the BrickHouse brand.

In our Q & A with Greg below, you'll get a sense of his thoughtful and insightful intelligence.

Q: What unique quality or qualities do you believe have made you successful both in life and in the band?

A: An ability and willingness to embrace change has probably contributed more to the modest successes I've enjoyed in life than other personal attributes. Moving fast and stopping quickly are important – no question. But life's path is never "straight-and-narrow," so it's how you handle the "curves" that usually matters most!

Q: What have you learned from your life experience

that you've brought to the band?

A: Communication of all kinds is a never-ending cycle of tension and release. Humor is a particularly potent form of release, and a liberal application of it is critical in the highly-charged, emotional-intellectual performance environment.

Q: What have you learned from your band / music experience that you've taken back into your life?

A: You're not who you say you are! I have met many musicians over the years whose social personas differ considerably from their musical personas. Because music is such an inferential and emotional form of communication, it's often easier to convey – or harder to conceal – feelings, attitudes, emotions and opinions when "speaking in music" than it is when using mere words.

Q: What do you value most about the other members of the band? What have you learned from them?

A: Ensemble-playing is a group endeavor, with all the challenges and rewards that come from several voices trying to convey one thought. For that effort to succeed, a band must ultimately function as an accepting and supporting "family" with the goal of meeting the needs of its family members. The Brickhouse Band is a particularly effective family unit, with significant variance in the experiences of its members, but with lots of genuine love and good-will expressed by each member for each member.

Q: What is your favorite band memory to this point? Any particularly humorous moment? Painful or embarrassing moment? Educational moment?

A: The most significant memory for me is my first rehearsal with the band. Often, musicians are pretty self-

absorbed, or maybe self-contained, during auditions. I've always been that way. But from almost the first note, the drive, power and musicality of The Brickhouse Band ensemble was undeniable. During that rehearsal, I had the eerie sensation of "hearing me play with the band," rather than just playing music with a group of strangers. It was one of those "the whole is greater than the sum of its parts" moments that make playing music in an ensemble setting so rewarding.

My other "favorite moment" is ongoing. It involves the enormous satisfaction of "nailing" a particularly challenging song. Our impressive ability to take on a wide variety of musical challenges is what makes The Brickhouse Band my favorite team sport!

Q: Do you have a particular philosophy of life that you embrace.

A: Only "no matter where you go, there you are." We truly have little control over the events that occur in our lives. What we do with those events when they "happen to us" is what defines us as individuals and ultimately determines our fate.

CHAPTER 5

Brand Yourself: Leverage Everything That Happens to You

BrickHouse Principle Number 5: You must leverage everything that happens to you.

Have you ever considered that everything that happens to you is an opportunity to practice? It might be an opportunity to practice patience. It might be an opportunity to practice endurance. It might be an opportunity to practice a new skill. Or it might even be an opportunity to practice compassionate love. The idea here is that if everything is considered practice, you can work to *leverage* everything that happens to you.

With this approach, you can get better at patience. You can improve your endurance. You can become more skillful and competent. You can remain awake to the chance to exercise compassion where you once felt contempt. After all, it's just an occasion to practice!

Consider that the strongest people are those who can turn everything to their advantage. Perhaps you know people like this. It's as if they come out of any situation, however bleak it seems, smelling like a rose. If so, it's not an accident. These people have trained themselves to immediately recognize the opportunity to leverage any situation.

Why is it useful to know how to leverage everything that happens? Because you learn to:

- *Leverage knowledge*. Learn from your mistakes.
- *Leverage attrition*. Upgrade with more highly-skilled personnel when people retire or leave.
- *Leverage contacts*. Write down the contact information of anyone who has even a remote interest in you or your business.
- *Leverage advertising opportunities*. Recognize that every moment is a selling opportunity.
- *Leverage what's already working*. Replicate what is working for others; don't reinvent the wheel.

Make everything work *for* you!

That sounds great. But how do you do it?

The BrickHouse Philosophy says, "In our world, nothing ever goes wrong."

"In my world, nothing ever goes wrong."

Wow, what a statement! That statement was made by a man named Nisargadatta Maharaj. Maharaj was a 20th century Indian teacher and philosopher. Most interpreters of his teachings would tell you that, with that statement, he was telling us to simply observe and accept everything that happens as part of life's unfolding. I would take it a step further. I believe you can intuit from his statement that if nothing ever goes wrong, that means something is always going right. It's up to you to figure out what that is. If you can, you can capitalize on everything that's happening.

Every day, begin the practice of asking, "How can I use what is happening to my advantage?"

How can I use this day to my advantage?

How can I use this situation to my advantage?

How can I use this assignment to my advantage?

How can I use this relationship to my advantage?

How can I use this problem to my advantage?

Asking a great question opens the space for a great answer. I guarantee you that people who emerge from every situation smelling like a rose ask the above questions consistently. This is how you leverage everything that happens. You ask how you can make it work *for* you. It's also quite acceptable to extend that question to how you can use this situation to benefit others. This takes you from the perception of a problem right into a potential solution. After all, your problems are opportunities to practice as well. They are a test of your ability to overcome whatever stress and pressure you believe they're bringing.

Now I can hear people challenging this idea. How do you make a diagnosis of cancer work for you or anyone else? How do you make coronary bypass surgery work for you? How do you make the death of a family member work for you? Believe me, I get it. Those are situations of enormous gravity and they carry all kinds of problems, grief and pain. It's quite possible that you won't be able to make them work for you. Most people don't and I don't blame them. *I'm simply suggesting that the option of asking how you might use a situation opens up some possibilities that might not have become apparent otherwise.*

If you are diagnosed with cancer, you may not find a ready answer to *how you can use this*. But you might. It might be that you use your situation as a research opportunity to test new medicines. This could benefit you as well as others down the road. It might be that you find an opportunity to teach your children and loved ones how to deal with such a challenging situation with grace and courage. Or it might simply be an opportunity to practice being bigger than whatever happens to you.

Perhaps the greatest example I ever saw of this came from a man named Daniel J. Youssi. Dan was one of the finest men I ever knew. We met while attending Illinois State University. He had grown up in a tiny Midwestern town with the unlikely name of Paw Paw, Illinois. When we met, Dan was attending college on the G.I. bill. He used to regale me with stories about being in the Army's 82nd Airborne while stationed over in Germany. He was a couple of years older and he seemed so wise to the ways of the world. He was good-looking, charismatic, athletic, and we became lifelong friends. We did everything together. We worked out in the weight room together. We jogged on the streets together. We double dated. We knew the absolute intimate details of each other's lives in a way that only best friends can.

At college we would go out carousing with the boys. On the way home we would stop and sing songs to girls in front of their dormitory windows. Somehow, the fact that it was sometimes five degrees below zero didn't discourage us. As silly as it seems in retrospect, the girls seemed to enjoy it and we thought we were pretty cool. And we loved to sing. Dan and I began one tradition that we continued each year on Christmas Eve. No matter where we were in the world and no matter what our life circumstance was, one of us would call the other and we would sing "O Holy Night" into the phone at the top of our lungs. I took the high harmony. It always cracked us up. We could barely get through it without laughing because after all, "O Holy Night" was the song that got me rescued from the Vietcong.

Yes, rescued from the Vietcong. *But it was just a dream*. Unlike Dan, I never even served in the military. I registered for the draft and would have gladly served if called. But college was my priority in the mid 70's. I have no idea where this dream came from or why I had it. But I dreamed that I had been captured in Vietnam. You know how strange dreams can be. While captured, it seemed I had no hope of escape. But somehow, I sensed that Dan and his airborne buddies were out looking to rescue me. So all of a sudden, I started belting out "O Holy Night" at the top of my lungs. As luck would have it, they heard me and were able to locate my position. They stormed the enemy camp and I was freed. When I told Dan and the guys at school about that dream, we made "O Holy Night" our official theme song. To this day, I can't hear it and not smile from the absolute absurdity of it all.

For the first ten years after college, Dan and I made a point to visit each other at least once a year. That usually meant one of us was flying across the country. When he got divorced, I flew out to give him some emotional support while he settled into a new place. He opted for a one bedroom apartment. He walked me up the stairs and flipped on the light switch. It was completely empty, not even a sleeping bag. I said, "I love what you've done with the place!" I think two months went by before he even got any furniture. Even though extremely successful in sales, he just didn't care about "stuff."

Eventually, he remarried and settled outside of San Diego. He would occasionally fly up to Seattle on business. While it was his charisma and strong work ethic that had made him incredibly successful, it was how he spent his free time that would become his legacy.

From the time I first met him, Dan had always been heavily into Bible study. He became a very strong Christian as he grew older. He didn't make a lot of noise about it, didn't proselytize or try and cram his religion down your throat. He just lived from his own moral grounding. For several years, he went into prisons and spoke with prisoners about his relationship with God and what it had done for him. Dan was a pretty tough guy so I suspect he was able to get their attention fairly readily. His reputation for the work he was doing both in the prison system and in the community was outstanding. He was a terrific speaker and always in high demand. He helped to change a number of lives for the better. I was always proud of him.

We used to talk a lot about life and death. But we talked about death as young people do, as something distant and unfamiliar. While he was more certain about a heavenly reward than I, we did agree that ultimately, how you died would be one of the most important statements you would ever make about who you are. We promised each other that when our time came, we would face death with bravery, humor and as much dignity as we could muster. When talking about death, we often referred to the Gordon Liddy quote that we introduced in chapter three, "Defeat the fear of death and welcome the death of fear." We loved the story of the time Liddy was leaving the courtroom before going to prison for his role as a Watergate conspirator. As he was being led away, Liddy turned to his attorney and said, "Tell them to watch closely. I'll show them how to die."

We loved those kinds of bold statements and before going into a tense situation, one of us would look at the other and say in a hushed and serious tone, "Tell them to watch closely, I'll show them how to die." We would immediately begin howling with laughter and whatever tension was looming was immediately defused.

Then, in December of 2004, I got an e-mail from Dan's wife Amy. It was titled "Dan's Recent Brain Surgery." I figured it was a joke. I just figured that Dan was going to be poking fun at himself for something silly he had done. Or maybe he would joke that someone had removed his brain. I was wrong. One night, Dan had been watching Monday night football. He bent over to pick something up off the floor. He woke up four days later in intensive care. They had found stage three tumors in his brain.

He told me that realistically, the doctors had given him three to six months to live. Or at least that was the average length of time people in his condition usually lasted. Not surprisingly, he lasted much longer. He faced death exactly as we had mentally rehearsed and planned some thirty years before. His courage and humor were a lesson to me and if I don't go quickly, I hope that I can show the same metal that he showed to the end.

To give you a sense of how he kept his spirit and used his situation, I've enclosed some of his e-mails. Because one of the tumors was pushing up against the portion of his brain controlling sight, he had difficulty seeing and typing. Dan was extremely articulate and had been an honor student in college. The mistakes and misspellings in the e-mails are simply an indication of what he was going through and how very sick he was. Yet he never complained. Not once. The saddest part of all was toward the very end. He would send e-mails in huge, size 48-font, but they were unintelligible because he just couldn't see any longer. It was heartbreaking. I would respond, acting as if I could actually read what he had written, hoping he wouldn't know the difference. I hoped that Amy might be reading my responses to him.

There will be references in the e-mails that you won't understand (e.g. "manning" – it's a term we used about how to act under adversity. There are also numerous references to bodybuilding and weight training). I enclose these e-mails not for the content but for what it shows about this man's attitude. These e-mails are poignant, yet upbeat. They show you how one great man responded to impending death with great character and courage.

Feb. 25, 2005

Greetings King of Power and Massiveness!

Here on the Western front things move in the positive and excited directions. I have, due to the medicines, lost all size and mass acquired under the bar. Weighing in at 148 pounds. Look even skinnier. Having said that, I have gotten them to drop the medicines that have caused the atrophy over the last few weeks and have started the long drive up. What is encouraging is if you know the way to get back to (90 pound bench press for 1 rep), and you can force the work, you'll get back to 185 times 4... it's just time and work. It's how we started King. I remember 150 pounds on the machine.

Honestly, King, I'm not going thru any fear, worrry, anxiety, nothing... I have had none since day one ever. Sleep like a log. Eating now like a pig, which is awesome,, my wife can cook! All my thoughts are what and where I'm heading us next. Tt you more later, friends always, Yous

April 25, 2005

king of size and massiveness. all here is great my life couldn't be better to be honest. i am off work and am napping like you wouldn't believe every day i put it down at 1pm for about a two to three hour shot! Meaning in the extremous. my wieghts are just atrocious but i do what id can. think i told you i can't bench 60 pounds bt today actualally succeeeded with four reps of 60 pounds so hey, I'm copetitive :)

i havve no pain other than fatigue. They tell 60% of those with my tumor cash it in the first six months, 90% croak within a year. They are telling me they think I'm cashing it being now and Valentines day. Me, I plan to live to be 70. i continue to man feriociously here. A good chance to share man principals. an epic crisis of non-manning the so cal area. I will repair this. how is the band doing. give me a ring sometime we'll catch. continue manning great northwest. So Cal Man, friends always, Yous (heard from 1/2 paw paw.

July 6, 2005

gregreetings man on power and mass.

king. all is great here. i have had no pain medicine since march. still llifting 60 pound bench for 4 reps today. enjoying life like never before. having a ball. never happier, calmer, more at peace. alreadijng beat the first kill zone for this thing (they say 80% who have my tumor die in first 6 months. I passed that in june. Hop;e alll is well with you and your fam king. maybe you'lll hit the real big time with the band before i croak. it. hi to brooke friends always, yous

Dan's response to his illness was to suck it up and try not to be a burden to those around him. Although he never directly stated it, I knew he was conscious of being watched. His wife, his children, and all of us who loved him were getting a lesson in how to conduct ourselves under the most extreme stress. He used his final days as a teaching opportunity. He drew his last breath on November 14th, 2005.

Everyone talks about people who teach them how to live. I already know how to live. Dan taught me how to die. With a spirit that never broke, he showed me how to use impending death as a vehicle to teach courage and care for others. When he realized that he couldn't change his situation, he adapted and changed himself.

I include this example only to show how one person

under extremely difficult circumstances answered the question, "How can I use this?" Dan used his ability to leverage his final days in a positive and constructive way. His memory always reminds me that I have the ability to choose my response to any situation. In remembering him, I try and examine every difficulty with an idea towards how any situation can be leveraged. After all, if he could face death in that manner, how can I possible fold up under much less duress? Dan was bigger than the ultimate challenge – death. In remembering his example, surely I can work to be bigger than whatever challenges I face.

Leveraging Towards Business Achievement

How does the manner in which one faces death relate to achievement in business? One would not normally equate the two. After all, facing a terminal illness puts a person under almost constant stress. While certainly not equivalent to the stress of impending death, people often interpret and internalize their business problems in a similar manner. In fact, many years ago a well-known study of what people perceived as stressful indicated that people feared public speaking even more than death. Imagine that. That says that people would rather be in the coffin than giving the eulogy!

To succeed, you must be able to leverage your opportunities, particularly when under duress. That means that you'll need to be able to think clearly even under chaotic circumstances. Otherwise, you won't see the opportunities. We already know that our thinking processes sometime shut down under pressure. If you're in an important business meeting and you are unexpectedly called upon to speak, you have an opportunity. If your mind shuts down, you will lose this unforeseen chance to shine.

When creditors are calling, customers are waiting, and employees are getting ready to stage a coup, you may feel like there is just too much commotion to think and act effectively. But like Sully, our U.S. Airways pilot from chapter three who kept his cool under extreme stress, chaos requires that you think under pressure. Then you must act. In an economic downturn, some people interpret their situation as if they might be facing death. They sometimes panic. They stop thinking about solving problems and what they need to get done. They get consumed with an awful fate that they convince themselves is certain. *The people who succeed will be the ones who in the face of stress, come up with a well-thought-out, skillful strategy and who act on it.*

Under duress, you *can think clearly and act purposefully*. After all, everyone faces the stress and pressure that comes with problems. You are no different. But like my friend Dan, you can work to become bigger than your problems. It's a fact that some people will let you down. Others will get caught up in personal agendas that have nothing to do with your chosen destination. There will be conflicts and disagreements. Some people may quit and you may in fact have to start over. But you're still here so you can! If you keep your mind active and in the game, you are much more apt to find a way to leverage anything that happens.

Leveraging business opportunities can be as simple as putting yourself in the customer's shoes in order to understand their need. For example, we're currently working with an organization of dentists who generously volunteer their services to assist 3rd world countries. Each year they have a silent auction to raise money, but they have a difficult time generating excitement around the event. After all, it's *silent*. There's no hype, no buzz, and no electricity around the wonderful items being auctioned off. People walk around in expensive tuxedos and suits and act in the kind of sophisticated manner that formal attire usually dictates.

Enter the BrickHouse Band. We recognize the need for a little excitement. This group needs to generate a party atmosphere. So this year, the organization is going with a 70's disco theme. People will be encouraged to dress in the silk shirts and outrageous disco costumes of the day. The band will perform immediately after dinner before people have the slightest impulse to leave. We will provide a complete floor show for those who would prefer to watch and not dance. But the dancers will have their due as well. More importantly, during the silent auction itself, which will take place before dinner, we'll have our three attractive female singers/dancers take on different characters and personalities. While wearing wireless microphones, they'll actually go up to people, interview them, tell them about the items being auctioned and just generally create excitement unlike anything this group has ever seen. Each auction item will get featured and you can bet that this charity event will raise unprecedented money.

The BrickHouse Philosophy says, "First, you must get their attention."

The fact that corporate branding has become a business buzzword over the last decade doesn't make it any less significant. It's an important concept to manage. Whether deserved or not, your reputation with customers will become your brand. It is who and what your business is.

A business reputation is different from a personal reputation. Your personal reputation is in the hands of other people. If you meet five hundred people, you will have 500 reputations. Much of that is beyond your control. The only thing you can control is your character. That will always exist independently of your reputation.

In business it's different. It's essential to manage your reputation. That's simply because, without a good reputation, your business probably won't last. Essentially, your business character is equivalent to your business reputation because it's entirely in the perception of customers. Whatever the customer believes becomes the truth. For good or ill, your business reputation will become your brand. You must manage it by providing outstanding customer service. If you make a mistake and it becomes public, you must immediately rectify it publicly as well. Customers and potential customers must know that you are completely committed to their well being and that you will always make things right.

Marketing

Remember that we defined our customer as the person or entity that is paying you. If you are marketing to anyone other than your customer, you should consider why. Your marketing strategy should be aimed at your customer demographic. It should be designed around all of the wonderful reasons you are going to make them feel good on an emotional level.

At the highest level, your marketing strategy should be dictated by three key points:

1. Who you are and what you provide.
2. Who your customer is and their demographic characteristics (e.g., their age, gender, earning ability, spending habits, needs, desires, and accessibility)
3. The reason that they should buy you or your services

After a time, most businesses have a handle on who they are and what they provide. If they have done their vision and mission statements as referenced in chapter one, they know who they are and what they provide. The problem begins when they lose track of their demographic target audience. For example, while our band has a website, a MySpace page and a social networking presence, we don't spend much time there. Why? Our big paydays come from corporate and private events, conventions, large celebrations and high-end wedding receptions. In addition, we will also book through agents. As a result, it's not mandatory that we have a large following of people who frequent clubs and bars where live music is performed. While we very much enjoy playing those venues, their return on investment is simply not as great as corporate events. So we don't specifically market to that audience.

We see many bands spending tremendous amounts of energy cultivating a clientele that probably can't or won't hire them. It is absolutely imperative that your marketing have a focused target demographic that makes sense for your business. Otherwise you can get lost in the thousands of advertisements out there competing with you. Now if you are a band that is promoting original music and trying to sell CDs, you would need some popular support. Or if you were trying to sign with a record label, you would need to prove that you can build a following. But if you're a high-end cover band, the average John Q. Public isn't going to hire you. So if you're spending resources marketing to him, you should ask yourself why.

That's not to say the John Q. Public isn't important. Every moment with every person is a selling opportunity. And I'm not talking about a hard sell. I'm simply talking about being an outstanding representative of your product. Being kind and considerate on a daily basis to everyone you meet speaks well of your business and you. Being neat, clean and well-dressed whenever you're in public is never wrong. After all, you never know who you will meet that could help your business grow. That's why you need your elevator speech.

Your elevator speech will provide any prospective customer with a twenty second synopsis of who you are and what you do. Twenty seconds is about the time that it would take to ride up an elevator. Just recently, I had occasion to use mine. We were playing a convention at a downtown Seattle hotel. I was walking through the lobby in full band attire and a gentleman stopped me and said he liked my shirt. He asked about it and why I was wearing it. I gave him the elevator speech.

Oh, this shirt is part of my band outfit. My name is Lee Witt and I'm with the BrickHouse Band playing in the ballroom tonight. We're a Vegas style show band that delivers high energy dance music and a complete floor show. We primarily play corporate events, conventions, private celebrations and high-end wedding receptions. But recently we've branched out into other corporate services as well.

I then gave him a business card containing both our band and our consulting services website. These website outline our complete range of services. Had we had more time, I would have continued to elaborate and would have inquired about him. I would have asked him about what his does, where he does it and what his interests were. Everyone could be or could know a potential customer. A side benefit is that it's also fun just to get to know people.

Brooke and I chuckle at the surprised look on the faces of potential corporate clients when we first meet with them. I guess because they're looking to hire a band, they're expecting us to show up in tattoos and tee shirts. While we have nothing against tattoos and tee shirts, we find that our corporate clients appreciate that we arrive in formal business attire. We expect the same of any agent representation that we have working on our behalf. We bring a standard list of customer-oriented questions and of course, we listen closely to understand their requirements.

People want to buy from successful people. Brooke and I close over 90% of the customers that we meet with face-to-face. They feel our sincerity and by the time we leave them, they feel secure that their needs will be met. They know that they are hiring a company that has experience. They know that they are hiring people that care. It's not that Brooke and I are better than anyone else. But our product is. And we do our best to convey that to the customer. As such, we take the time to prepare. We show up polished and ready to serve the client. We really do give a damn.

Hype

It's important to spend a moment addressing hype because it's everywhere. And there's a reason for that. Like the BrickHouse philosophy says, "First, you must get their attention." From infomercials to billboards, it seems that you can't go anywhere without being inundated with advertising. Much of that advertising is very well packaged and extremely savvy. It takes advantage of the fact that as potential customers, *we want to believe*. I certainly do. I want to believe that all of these products will make me healthy, wealthy and wise. And most likely some of them will. But many of them won't.

Perhaps the key to success in the coming years will be your ability to fuel your own hype without buying in to the over-inflated assertions of others. In an ultra-competitive world, potential customers need to know you exist. So you must somehow get their attention. These days, that means hype. We're not going to tell you how to hype your individual business. That's because every business is different. However, we will suggest that you display your strengths and the qualities that differentiate you from your competition in a way that can be *seen* by potential customers who can afford to pay you.

Most importantly, an outstanding product must be at the core of your hype. Otherwise, hype won't matter. You will be found out. You will be exposed as a fraud. Hype without substance will not work in the long run. And really, why would you want it to? Remember, you're in business to serve customers and compete to win! That means being the best you can be.

Branding and Branching Out

After several years of hard work, the BrickHouse name has now become a brand of its own. On the West Coast, the name has become synonymous with high-quality, fun, interactive entertainment. We have now capitalized on our name by branching out into other areas where we are strong. While band services can still be found at www.brickhouseband.com – we also offer a new range of services under the BrickHouse brand at the www.brickhouseleadership.com website. This has enabled us to go national and serve more customers while reaching more people with our performance methodology. We love the life we've created and we are dedicated to helping others do the same.

The BrickHouse Philosophy says, "Leverage Time."

Time is the one thing you can't get back. As such, I feel strongly about it. In fact, some of you are going to be put off reading this section. I'm betting some of you won't finish it. It's going to hurt. It's going to seem like I'm scolding you. But I encourage you to be open-minded and read this section anyway. I'm intentionally not sugar-coating this. I'm going to seem a little combative but my feeling is that in this case, it's warranted. I'm using the pronoun "you" to make this a strong message. If you think I'm speaking to you as you read this, just absorb the material and see if it makes sense. If you don't think it applies to you, minimally, you'll probably be entertained.

How often do we hear people say that they don't have enough time – or that they ran out of time – or that time got away from them?

In reality, we all have the same amount of time. We all get the same twenty-four hours. While some people are using lack of time as an excuse, others are using time to advance towards their destinations.

It might be useful to stop telling yourself that there isn't enough time. There is as much time as there is. Back in about 50 A.D., the great Roman orator, Seneca, said that the gods had been quite generous with time but that people made poor use of it. Now how could Seneca possibly understand? After all, he didn't have cable. He didn't have a flat plasma screen with high definition. He didn't have e-mail, twitter, two careers and three cell phones.

That's true. Seneca didn't have any of the thousands of distractions competing for your attention. But the fact that people made poor use of time even then means one thing. If you're struggling with time, time isn't the problem. *You are*. As Seneca suggested, you can't change how much time you have, you can only change the ways that you use it. Using it to your advantage is how you leverage time.

If you feel overwhelmed, out of control and always behind, you may want to reevaluate your relationship with time. In a cause and effect universe, you may be sabotaging yourself. Could it possibly be that you sometimes need to say no? Saying no is difficult in a world with so much opportunity. There's a lot of cool stuff to do. Saying no to potentially great opportunities can be excruciating. I've done it and I'll bet you have as well. It hurts, it's painful, but sometimes you simply have to say no because saying yes to something you don't have time to deliver is even more painful.

Brooke and I have had to say no to vacation opportunities and family functions. Why? Because we've said yes to band opportunities. At the same time, we've said no to band opportunities because we've said yes to our children or other career commitments. It's not easy making these choices. But if you say yes to one thing, you may have to say no to another. *No is always an option*.

While learning to say no, you may also want to change the way that you think about time. Begin by getting rid of the inner dialogue that says you don't have enough. Telling yourself that you don't have enough time just becomes a self-fulfilling prophecy. I'll occasionally catch myself saying, "I wish there were more hours in a day." But this cannot become my mantra. If it does, everything soon becomes a crisis. I'll convince myself I'm in a state of overwhelm. When that happens, everything becomes an emergency.

So what should we do?

Here is where all of the time management gurus would lay out all of the helpful hints about how to manage time. They would tell you to write everything down, make a list, prioritize the list, put time constraints on each item and then plan your week and month from there.

Those are excellent things to do. I do them; I think you should too. *But this isn't really about making a list and prioritizing the list.* You already know that you should be doing those things. Don't you? Of course you do. Let's cut to the quick. We can simplify this. It's just that some of you don't want to. You don't want to simplify it. You enjoy the chaos. You like having a built-in excuse for always being late. You like having an excuse for not getting things done. Some of you even like the adrenaline rush of always being frantic. Others like using their time to work on the wrong thing because it's easier or more fun than working on the right thing.

Well - STOP IT!

Seriously, stop it. The rest of us don't care that you don't have enough time. We don't. We live in the same world as you do. You are not unique. The world isn't conspiring against you any more than it is the rest of us. The fact is, you chose to work on the wrong thing. Or you said yes when you should have said no. Or you inaccurately assessed that you could do twenty-seven things by 5:00 p.m. You took on more work or more responsibilities or more fun when *you should have known better*. The fact is – you love the busyness. Otherwise, why would you make a list with too many things to complete? You're smarter than that. So there must be something in it for you. You must love it or you wouldn't do it, week after week, month after month, year after year. If it was as painful as you say, you'd change.

Now you may be thinking, *why is this guy scolding me? My life is tough enough without him yelling at me for being too busy. He doesn't know anything about my life. He doesn't understand my situation. I don't need this.*

YES, YOU DO! You need it big-time. You need it precisely because your life *is* tough. Even worse, you're making life tougher for everyone around you. You're telling people you're going to complete things and then you don't. You tell people you're going to be somewhere and then you're late if you even get there at all. And you've always got the excuse of being too busy. After all, there's not enough time!

If that's true, how did everyone else get there?

Oh, that's right. It's different for you. You're special. You are more important than other people. That's what you're telling them with your behavior whenever you make them wait. You're saying *I'm more important than you!*

Look, here's why I'm giving you this virtual spanking. I don't want your life to be tougher; I want it to be easier. No, actually, that's not true. I don't care if it's easier. It probably won't be. *I care that it's more productive*. I care that you get a shot at being successful in something you really want to achieve. I care that you learn how to take an idea and make it an amazing reality. That's what I want for you – and I'd prefer you do it without abusing other people's time in the process.

So what am I supposed to do you ask? I'll tell you. But first, let me follow your question with a question. If the suggestions from the time management gurus aren't working for you, why do you think that is?

If you're struggling with the answer, here it is. Because this isn't about making a list and setting priorities. This is about waking up and growing up. You're not a teenager any more. Just because something would be a cool thing to do doesn't mean you've got time to do it! The coolness of it is not the issue. The amount of time you have is the issue. This is about being a responsible adult. This is about accepting responsibility for your own circumstances and choices. Sometimes it just boils down to this...*you can have this – or you can have that! You can't have both, at least not at the same time!*

I hear you. *You want it all!* I know. I want it all too. But at some point, I have to pretend I'm mature enough to accept responsibility for the choices I make. That means that I can't have it all at the same time.

This is as true in small things as it is in big things.

> *Small thing* – I can read this book or I can watch the ball game.
>
> *Big thing* – I can decide to have children and raise them properly or I can decide that I have other priorities I'd like to pursue that preclude having kids.

These are the kinds of choices that everyone faces. But what people sometimes don't face is that each choice has a consequence. If you choose *this*, it means you haven't chosen *that*! You can't go to college, have a full time job, raise children, watch TV, be in a band, work out five days a week, and go party on Friday and Saturday night.

You might have a go at doing all of that – but you won't do it successfully. Time will not allow it. And you'll leave a lot of innocent bodies in your wake. When the band first began, one of our female leads was our niece, Kerri. She earned my utmost respect the day that she walked into rehearsal and without a lot of drama, simply said that she couldn't apply her best efforts to her college studies, keep the part time job that she needed, and do justice to the band. Therefore, she had to leave the band.

God bless her, I had no problem with this. She was

only about 22 at the time and I respected the maturity of her decision. This was especially true because I knew the band was important to her. But she prioritized her education and the money she needed for that over the fun of the band. It was the right thing to do and I admired her for it.

Yes, by not choosing everything, you'll miss some opportunities. I've missed plenty. But in saying no to certain opportunities, you can properly say yes to others. Perhaps more importantly, you'll become more honorable in meeting the commitments you've made. People will be able to trust you. If you can't be on time, they can't trust you. If you promise to deliver something yet people are making contingency plans in case you don't, *they don't trust you*. They may understand that you have the best intentions on delivering – but if they know you to be a person who struggles with time, they have to plan for the worst. So they're making a backup plan as we speak because they've been burned by you before.

That's not to say that you weren't sorry. Damn straight you were. You felt badly about it. But apparently you didn't feel badly enough about it to change. Otherwise you wouldn't be so mad at me right now.

Unlike the people who are mad, the people who keep their commitments and don't over-schedule are all smiling as they read this. They're yelling, "Right on, brother! Tell it like it is!"

You see, this isn't just about you. It's about the chaotic chain of events you set in motion whenever you over-commit. You cost your company, your family, your friends and everyone who relies on you when you don't leverage time properly. When you over-commit, they have to cover for you and they're probably growing weary.

If you aren't one of these people, I'll bet you know some. Just like you, some people are as good as gold when they tell you something. You can bank it. You never have to plan contingencies with them because their word is solid. These people know how to leverage time.

Of course, the great irony is; you'll get more of what you want in the long run by not over-committing, over-scheduling and over-working yourself. You'll actually complete more when you scale back, stop multi-tasking, get off the phone and complete the task in front of you. When that's complete, you can move on to the next thing – and the one after that. You might be amazed at what you get done.

Am I suggesting you never talk on the phone? No, of course not. I'm suggesting you talk when it makes business sense for you – or when common courtesy dictates it. Good business may mean you need to spend a lot of time on the phone and that's fine. It may also mean that you check messages and return calls promptly. Be strategic. Customer calls should be taken or returned immediately. Otherwise, you'll get more done by devoting time for the phone and e-mail when it fits into *your* schedule. It's your agenda. Take charge of it and don't let it take charge of you.

Bang for Your Buck

You can make the decision to do the things worth doing. *You know what they are*. People who leverage time spend time on the things that give them the greatest return on investment. They get the most bang for their buck. They spend the majority of time on the activities that delight customers and bring in revenue.

At times, the things that bring in the most revenue may not be the things that are the most fun. What is actually important? What must be done even if it's tedious or unpleasant? Your ability to suspend your discomfort long enough to get something done that's not necessarily fun will go a long way towards making you successful. People convince themselves that something they enjoy doing out-prioritizes something they want to avoid. They do this even when they know the unpleasant task is more important. We don't want to do it so we put it off. But we have to do it. We can't advance until we do. Successful people do the things that are uncomfortable. Successful people do the things that unsuccessful people just will not do.

So just how do you identify your real priorities? How do you revisit your destination if you feel it may be changing or you're no longer certain of our vision and mission?

How to Identify the True Priorities

1) *Stop!*

   Go to your office alone. Sit down. Shut the phone off. Be quiet. Breathe.

2) *Visit the bottom line and identify your business destination?*

   Ask yourself, "What is the purpose of this business? What product brings in revenue and who is the customer?"

3) *Gather the key members of your management team and verify your answer.*

   Share your answers to number two and see if your managers agree. Converse until you all agree upon the purpose; that is, who you are serving and what is making you money. This is not about what everyone *likes* to do. It's about what you do that makes money for the business.

4) *Get everything out of the way of your destination.*

   Once you agree upon the destination, remove any activity that is not all about it. If what you're doing isn't supporting your product and customer, why you are doing it? Identify the non-value added activities and stop doing them.

5) *Home in on your destination and execute.*

   Your destination is not your fancy new production machinery. It is not your nice clean new office. It is not your cool stationery and business cards. It is not phone calls, meetings, and continuous conversation about your product or service. *You reach your destination when you are producing an outstanding product for a satisfied customer and you are collecting the receivables.* Doing this keeps you in the phone book.

Once you've established your true priorities, it's still easy to get trapped into telling ourselves *I shouldn't have to do this*. But that thought isn't relevant to getting it done. At some point you have to *man up* or *woman up*! It may not be fair. Other people may be out having fun while you're working. But your willingness to step up to the task is what will make you extraordinary in a world where most people are average.

Leveraging time sometimes means that you must attempt to see with new eyes. Revisit how you spend time and monitor your progress daily.

One of the best ways of leveraging time is in the management of exercise and nutrition. Nothing gives you a bang-for-your-buck like exercise and healthy eating because they allow you to succeed within our next philosophical maxim.

The BrickHouse Philosophy says, "Leverage Energy"

Perhaps even more important than leveraging time is leveraging energy. Time won't serve you if you don't have the energy and good health to use it. That's why effectively and efficiently managing exercise, nutrition and rest is essential to reaching any destination. Physical vitality allows us to push through barriers. If you work full time and are a parent, you already have strenuous demands on your energy. If you add in extra-curricular activities, a second job and a social life, you're going to need every ounce of strength you can get.

Energy and vitality are indicators of great health. They are the fuel that can give your team another competitive advantage. Without them, it is difficult to create extraordinary results. In addition, energy is more than physical. Emotional energy rubs off on your customers. They feel it when your team brings it and they always want more of it. Outstanding customer service begins with the energy of the people who deliver the product.

Don't beat yourself up if you're tired and out of shape. There are studies that suggest that sixty-seven percent of American adults are currently overweight or obese. If the trend continues, that will rise to 86% within another few years. Even our pets are obese! So if you're feeling like you need to drop some weight, you're not alone. We can fix this. The *Always Advance* attitude suggests that we start from wherever we're at and improve from there.

Fast food, a sedentary lifestyle, and lives of convenience have helped to create a society that is largely unhealthy. While living in this unhealthy culture, your challenge is to create a healthy culture for yourself. This may make you unpopular because obviously, you'll be going against the grain. But you can do it. After all, without good health and the energy that comes from that, you will never accomplish all that you are capable of.

The interesting thing is that *we know what to do!* The information is out there. A formula of strength training, cardio work, proper nutrition and rest will create a healthy, fit, and energetic human. We know this.

So the question becomes, why are we not succeeding in implementing what we know? Why are we still obese when the television airwaves inundate us with infomercials touting exercise regimens and equipment, diets, juicers, and all kinds of motivation? Why are we not succeeding when libraries and bookstores are full of literature and videos telling us what to do?

There are probably a number of different answers to this question. You may have heard or even used some of them:

I'm bored with exercise. I'm tired. It's hard. It hurts. It's not convenient. I'm in a new relationship and I'm too busy. I hate dieting. I'm on vacation. It won't work for me; I have a slow metabolism. I have a new baby. I have a new job. My shoulder hurts. I need new workout clothes. I can't resist a great chocolate cake.

What's the common denominator among these answers?

They're all excuses. They are simple excuses for not doing what we know would be good for us. Whenever you do not act in your own best interests, you've probably created a story around why you can't do what you know would be healthy. Remember, as we learned in chapter three, there are only three things keeping you from what you want...skill, courage and resolve.

The *Always Advance* methodology can help you with all three. After all, if you don't make time for cultivating the energy that comes from health and fitness, you'll have to make time for illness and fatigue. And who has time for that?

BrickHouse has a simple system designed to give you the skill, the courage and perhaps most importantly, the resolve to keep you advancing in energy, health and fitness. It doesn't take a tremendous amount of time. This is good news because if you're like most folks, you don't have much time to spare. But it's not a five minute a day fix either. Our program is realistic, practical, doable and proven to work. *But only if you actually do it!* We're here for you if you think you need a helping hand. But ultimately, you'll have to take a look at the end of your own arm because taking care of yourself is your responsibility. At the end of the day, you are the one who must eat and exercise intelligently.

As you begin, you have to determine something. You must determine whether you are *interested* in being healthy and having energy or if you're *resolved* to be healthy and have energy. There's a difference. If you're interested in it, you might talk yourself out of that morning jog if it's raining. If you're resolved, you'll simply grab the rain gear and take off running. When you have resolve, it means you will reach your destination no matter what. You tolerate no excuses from yourself.

It's also important to note that, as we suggested in chapter two, there are people who will tell you whatever you want to hear in order to sell you something. Be wary of the shortcut mentality. The "eat anything you want, exercise only a few minutes a day" plans are designed to appeal to that part of you that wants something for nothing. But anything worthwhile usually comes with a price. Your health and energy are worth whatever price you have to pay. If you don't believe that, talk with someone who is confined to an iron lung. They would probably trade places with you in a heartbeat.

Our method advocates taking a look at your lifestyle in order to implement changes that you can live with for a lifetime. Quick fixes are not the answer for the long haul. They might help you temporarily, but ultimately, you are going to have to find a way to eat less, eat better, and exercise more. And you need to be smart about it. As such, I recommend you begin with a complete physical exam and a consultation with your physician before beginning any exercise and nutrition regimen. I also recommend that you consider changing your identity. No, not changing the name on your driver's license. I'm talking about changing your idea of the person you think you are and the labels you use for yourself.

Change Your Identity

Before getting into the specifics of nutrition and exercise, please consider this. There are all kinds of diets and exercise programs out there. Many of them have worked for a large number of people. But few of them have worked for those same people over an extended period of time. If you are one of those people, it might be useful to consider changing your identity. If you think you're a fat person on a diet, you'll still believe you're a fat person who has simply lost weight if you're successful. As a result, eventually, you'll go back to being that fat person. Why? Because that's who you believe you are.

Why not become a different person. Change your identity. Become a normally-weighted fit person who had previously been overweight. After all, that's the truth! Chances are that you weren't born overweight. You are a just a normal person who got big. So now I'm asking you to see the real you, a normally-weighted healthy person. I'm asking you to understand, believe and know that in fact, *you are not an overweight person*! You have simply made some choices that have gotten you to this point. Now, you're going to go back to the real you and stay there.

Most people unconsciously try and live up to their identity, even if their identity is not the ideal one. Begin thinking of yourself as the ideal you. Give yourself a new identity. You'll be much more apt to succeed.

Nutrition

Most of our food consumption in the United States revolves around red and processed meats, high-fat dairy products, refined flours, butter, french fries and tons of sugar. Typically, we don't eat enough fruits and vegetables. As such, we in the U.S. suffer high rates of diabetes, cancer, and cardiovascular disease. Other afflictions such as Alzheimer's disease that come with age may also be related to our diets.

If changing our dietary habits was easy, America wouldn't be overweight. It's not easy. In addition, it takes great awareness of what you're doing in the present moment when you're about to make an eating decision that doesn't serve you. Again, the mindfulness meditation practice we learned about in chapter four can help you stay aware and awake to what you're doing. It is designed to bring your mind into the present moment. Fortunately, that's where all of your decisions are made. They are all made in the present. When you lose awareness, it becomes easy to just grab something and shove it into your mouth. In our abundant society, food is everywhere. But you no longer need to grab it.

You can begin to make new choices beginning right now. You don't need to eat that piece of cheesecake right this second. It's easy to say no in the present moment. It's difficult to say no forever. So just say no for now and revisit whether you still want that cheesecake in twenty minutes. In twenty minutes, that will become the present moment and you can make the same "not eat the cheesecake right now" decision that you did twenty minutes ago. Once you've strung a number of these healthy present moment decisions together, you've begun to make great strides towards weight loss and greater energy.

This may sound crazy but it's very simple and effective.

It doesn't get promoted in television infomercials because it costs nothing. If you don't believe that you are a particularly disciplined person, it works because you don't have to be. We tend to think that discipline means self-denial over a long period of time. As such, we don't believe that we'll be able to maintain healthy eating and exercise habits into the future. But you don't live in the future and you don't have to have discipline tomorrow. You only need the mental resolve to not make an unhealthy eating choice right now. *This you can do!*

You have all the discipline and resolve you need in this moment. In this moment, you are completely capable of eating something healthy or not eating something unhealthy. But you might think, what's the point? I'll just blow it tomorrow. No, tomorrow is just a figment of your imagination. You can't live tomorrow. It doesn't exist. You can only live right now. Just make the right choice in this second.

If you absolutely cannot say no after a twenty minute wait, go ahead and eat the cheesecake. *But eat it mindfully*. Be aware of eating it and what you are doing to yourself. Afterwards, don't say, "Oh I've screwed up, I might as well just eat whatever I want." NO! Bring yourself back to the present and resolve to make a healthy choice in this *new* present moment. Right here and now. Tomorrow will take care of itself. You will be amazed at the progress you can make if you simply live in the now.

So how can we make this even easier? First, identify one or two kinds of vegetables that you will actually eat. Do the same with fruits. Second, take a piece of paper and draw a line down the middle. On one side, write down the snacks you typically eat. On the other side, write down a fruit or vegetable that you will substitute for that snack. You can also include plain, low-salt rice cakes or unbuttered popcorn occasionally.

Next, stop buying junk at grocery and convenience stores. There is a reason they call it "super-sized." It's designed to make you just that. I advocate lean meat, skinless chicken and fish as protein sources. Think of it this way; the more legs it has, the less of it you should eat. Beef and pork have four legs; eat them sparingly. Chicken and turkey have two legs. That's better. Best of all is fish. They have no legs. Make fish your protein staple.

Whole grain foods at most meals are fine as well; just don't overdo it. Get rid of fried foods and saturated fats. Get rid of trans-fats like those you find in cookies and potato chips. Make your fats the healthy ones. Olive oil, fish oil and other monounsaturated fats are fine in moderation. Nuts are also a healthier way to get fat into your diet. Always read food packaging labels; they will tell you the fat, carbohydrate, protein and sugar content of what you're eating.

Let's face it. If you are over ten years old, you probably know what you should and should not be eating. These days they even teach healthy eating habits in grammar school. Say yes to the apple, say no to the cookie. Say yes to the baked salmon, say no to the fried chicken cooked in lard. Sometimes we make this harder than it has to be. When it comes to food, what either goes in goes on or goes out. You're either wearing it, eliminating it, or burning it off.

If you need to count calories and it helps you, count

them. But make your calories count. Eat foods that are rich in nutritious value. Otherwise, you are eating empty calories that simply do harm. Here is a sample of what we consider healthy foods for each meal.

Breakfast Options:

Oatmeal
Fruit
Toast (dry is best but there are butter substitutes that you might consider)
Eggs with yolks (one day per week; egg whites are fine anytime)
Egg white omelet (cheese only in moderation)
Fat-free yogurt

Lunch Options:

Tuna, turkey, or chicken breast sandwich on whole wheat bread (or pita bread occasionally) with lettuce and tomato (no mayo, butter or margarine)
Any fruits and vegetables
Fat-free, low-salt rice cakes or pretzels

Dinner Options:

Skinless chicken breast or baked salmon
Any vegetables
Dry baked potato (no sour cream or butter)
For dessert, go for a walk with a loved one.

Snacking throughout the day is fine as long as you eat healthy snacks. It's better to eat small amounts throughout the day to keep your blood sugar from spiking. This also keeps your metabolic furnace running. In addition, it's easier to digest smaller amounts of food. Brooke and I are also big fans of protein shakes. They are a great way to help you meet your nutritional requirements without adding a lot of calories.

If you don't eat breakfast or lunch, you'll end up binging in the evening. Binging is not a sound nutrition plan. Plus, there are studies that show that eating only once a day will trick your body into thinking it's starving the rest of the time. This will cause your body to want to hold onto the food you do eat and store it as fat. Eating once a day is a bad idea.

If food is really a challenge for you, you might do well to consult a nutritionist. But this section gives you a sense of what we advocate for healthy long-term eating. Remember, you only have to make an appropriate eating choice right now, not later. You also know that without good health, you will never accomplish all that you are capable of. Proper nutrition is critical. Combine it with intelligently applied exercise and you will be well on your way to a destination of terrific health and energy.

Exercise

I don't think of exercise as a chore. It's like adult playtime to me. I love it. But like you, I'm extremely busy, so I've resolved to be healthy. I've exercised a minimum of three to six hours per week for thirty-five years.

Make exercise a priority. Put it on your calendar. Make an appointment with yourself at least three days a week to exercise. Four or five is better but three will do. Keep those sacred appointments just as you would a meeting with your boss. In reality, they are just as important.

As a person who has been involved with strength training and competitive powerlifting almost all of my life, I have a bias towards the benefits of weight training. I believe that there is nothing in life that gives you a better return on investment. The closest thing to the fountain of youth can be found in the weight room. You can see and feel your body getting stronger. It's observable. It's measurable. And you can make progress in as little as three hours per week. Given that there are 168 hours in a week, three hours does not seem disproportionate. You could split that time up as three 1-hour sessions or four, 45-minute sessions, depending on your schedule and preference.

Even as recently as ten years ago when I received personal training certification, weight training was almost always mentioned as an afterthought. Aerobic or cardio conditioning was believed to be the magic elixir for longevity and health. In reality, a sound health and fitness regimen includes both. Muscular strength and heart health go hand in hand. In fact, research over the last two decades has shown that men with the highest levels of strength were less likely to die from heart disease, cancer or any other cause. Being strong *is* heart healthy. A 19-year study cited in the *British Medical Journal* and conducted at the Dallas Aerobics Institute looked at 8,762 men between the ages of 20 and 80. Results showed that greater strength reduced the risk of death by cancer 32% and heart attack by 50%.

Strength training builds muscle. When you have greater muscle mass, you burn more calories, even at rest. If you combine just three hours per week of strength training workouts with proper nutrition, you can begin to change your body composition. You should also include proper rest to allow your body to recover. If you include stretching for five to ten minutes after your workout, you can increase your body's flexibility, the lack of which is a prime measure of aging.

Strength training also increases bone density. Many women face osteoporosis as they age. Weight training and enough calcium in your diet can offset this. The benefits of strength training are undeniable. If you get nothing else from this book, I hope you begin training with weights immediately, if you don't already. It is truly life-altering.

A balanced exercise program also includes aerobic training. Running, walking, climbing stairs, bicycling and rowing all qualify as aerobic conditioners. You can also purchase cardio equipment like treadmills and elliptical trainers or use the ones at a local gym. You can perform your cardio after your weight training session, or even on an alternate day. How much should you do? Well, I believe that many people over-train. Or at least they train to where they get to a point of diminishing returns. If you are truly tight on time, I believe that you can make great progress with a 15 to 20 minute cardio workout. Instead of training longer, push yourself more in that 15 to 20 minute window. Unless you are training to run a marathon, running for an hour is just killing time and putting stress on your joints. If it's more comfortable for you to train longer and easier, that's fine. For me, time is so precious that I'm trying to get the most benefit out of the least amount of time spent.

The most important thing is to make the time to exercise. The best time to do it is whenever you will. It doesn't so much matter whether you train in the morning, afternoon or evening. It simply matters that you do it. The rewards you will reap in terms of energy and health cannot be adequately quantified. In order to reach a great destination, you will need the kind of energy that only proper exercise and nutrition can provide.

Below are the BrickHouse Exercise Principles with a sample workout included. There are several great books and videos on training that you can buy or grab at the library. You might also consider hiring a personal trainer. Or you can contact us through our website for a free consultation. (www.brickhouseband.com)

BrickHouse Exercise Principles

- 45 minutes of weights – only 30 to 60 seconds of rest between sets.
- 15 - 20 minutes of cardio.
- Ascending sets when weight training: Very light weight up to heaviest. This provides a warm-up for each exercise.
- Change exercises every four to six weeks. Your body will adapt to any stress so you need a variety of exercises to avoid stagnation and grow.
- No body parts worked on consecutive days. You must allow time for growth and recovery.

Below is a sample beginning weight training program split over 4 days. A repetition (rep) is one movement. A set is a series of those repetitions. For example, one set of bench presses might include eight repetitions of the movement. You can perform 15 to 20 minutes of cardio at the end of each workout, or on the off days.

<u>Monday</u> (Chest, Shoulders, Triceps and Abs)

Chest

- Flat Bench Press – 3 sets of 8 to 15 repetitions
- Lying Flyes – 3 sets of 8 to 15 reps

Shoulders

- Lateral Raises with Dumbbells – 3 sets of 10 to 12 reps
- Military (Overhead) Press – 3 sets of 8 to 15 reps

Triceps

- Triceps Pushdowns – 3 sets of 8 to 12 reps
- Triceps Kickbacks with Dumbbells – 2 sets of 8 to 12 reps

Abdominals

- Ab Crunches to failure (as many as you can do) – 2 sets

<u>Wednesday</u> (Legs, Back and Biceps)

Legs

- Bodyweight Squats (warm-up) 1 set of 12 reps
- Barbell (or Dumbbell) squats 3 sets of 10 to 15 reps
- Lunges with Dumbbells – 2 sets of 10 to 15 reps

Back

- Barbell Rowing – 4 sets of 8 to 15 reps
- Deadlift – 2 sets of 10 to 15 reps

Biceps

- Barbell Curls – 3 sets of 8 to 15 reps
- Concentration Curl with Dumbbell – 2 sets of 10 reps

<u>Friday</u> (Chest, Shoulders, Triceps and Abs)

Chest

- Incline Dumbbell Press – 3 sets of 8 to 15 reps
- Incline Flyes – 3 sets of 8 to 15 reps

Shoulders

- Bent Lateral Raises with Dumbbells – 3 sets of 8 to 12 reps
- Front Dumbbell Raises – 3 sets of 8 to 12 reps

Triceps

- Dips (or close-grip pushups if dipping bar is not available) to failure – 2 sets
- Tricep Pushdowns – 3 sets of 8 to 12 reps

<u>Saturday</u> (Legs, Back and Biceps)

Legs

- Leg Extensions (if machine is available) – 3 sets of 10 to 15 reps
- Leg Curls (if machine is available) 3 sets of 10 to 15 reps

If neither machine is available, perform Squats – 3 sets of 6 to 8 reps

Back

- Pulldowns (if machine is available) – 3 sets of 10 to 15 reps

If machine is not available, perform Barbell Rowing – 4 sets of 6 to 8 reps

- Deadlift – 2 sets of 8 reps

Biceps

- Seated Dumbbell Curls – 3 sets of 8 to 10 reps
- Pull-ups (if chinning bar is available) – 2 sets to failure

You should be able to complete these workouts in 45 minutes or less. Always begin with a lighter weight and work up to heavier weights. Warming up prevents injury. Avoid injury at all cost because it's difficult to advance when injured.

If you perform your cardio after your weight routine, you can finish in about one hour. Taking care of yourself will only make you better and your business better. In addition, you set a great example for your family and colleagues. Take care of your body; you can't trade it in on a new one.

People who successfully brand their product know how to leverage everything that happens to them. They are never victims. They take charge of their actions and their attitudes. They take charge of their time and they manage their energy. In doing so, they take responsibility for everything that happens to them – and that's what winners do.

Key Points from Chapter Five

- Everything that happens can be leveraged to your advantage. Everything provides you with an opportunity to practice improvement.
- Market to a customer demographic that can actually hire and pay you. Then manage your brand by providing a great product with outstanding customer service.
- Master your elevator speech so that you never lose an opportunity to promote your products and services. Anyone could be or could know a potential customer.
- Manage and leverage your time by recognizing that you can either have this – or you can have that. But you can't have it all at the same time.
- Manage and leverage your energy by committing to an intelligent nutrition and exercise plan. We know what to do. We simply need to stop making excuses for not acting in our own best interests.
- Live in the present moment and make your healthy choices in the here and now. You don't have to worry about being disciplined tomorrow. For just this one second, you can be resolute.
- Weight training is the closest thing there is to the fountain of youth. Commit a minimum of three hours a week to weight training and you will not be disappointed.

KRISTI EVANS – Vocals and Dance

Courtesy of Lumina Photography

Sometimes incredibly good things come in small packages. Kristi Evans is one of those things. While small in stature, she is big in presence. Like many successful performers, Kristi is beautiful, smart, talented and hip. But unlike many, she has a quick-witted sense of humor that makes you whip your head around and ask, "Did she just say what I think she did?"

Having been an actress for several years, Kristi has

honed her improvisational chops to where she can turn into a "character" at any moment. Soon, everyone within earshot is laughing hysterically. We profile her in this chapter because Kristi embodies the spirit of "leveraging everything" that happens to her. She manages to successfully juggle work, school, acting and her music career into a schedule that would bring most people to their knees. Yet she powers on with a tough, spirited energy that enchants and charms everyone she meets.

Recently, while filming a pilot for a situation comedy, she suffered a serious injury to her hand. Most of us would have passed out from the pain or gone into shock. Not Kristi. She called from the hospital while *getting the tip of her finger reattached to her hand!* You can bet that she's already figuring out how to use this painful experience and somehow turn it to her advantage.

Kristi's vocal and dance talents have become an integral part of the BrickHouse stage show. She has an edgy, "can't take your eyes off of her" quality that has made her a fan favorite. We all can't wait to see what she's going to do next. Her star burns bright, and it's just the beginning.

We learn a little more about just what makes Kristi tick in our Q & A.

Q: What unique quality or qualities do you believe have made you successful both in life and in the band?

A: Organizational skills, a love of dressing fancy, and the ability to pinpoint what is ridiculous in life and enjoy it rather than condemn it. I also find that an innate fear of authority figures really gets the job done.

Q: What have you learned from your life experience that you've brought to the band?

A: One of my theater instructors continually said to me, "It's not about you, it's about the play," meaning, get rid of your ego and perform for the good of the collective. The play will stink, and YOU will stink if you are worried about making yourself look good.

Q: What have you learned from your band / music experience that you've taken back into your life?

A: Men enjoy provocative outfits. And, "It's not about you, it's about the play!" The Brickhouse Band teaches me that over and over again, and I mean really rams in it there, that you ONLY look good if you are making everyone around you look better.

Q: What do you value most about the other members of the band? What have you learned from them?

A: Good hearts are all around you.

Q: What is your favorite band memory to this point? Any particularly humorous moment? Painful or embarrassing moment? Educational moment?

A: Right now my favorite band memory is seeing my friends dancing and smiling like crazy people when they attended one of our shows. My friends don't get to see many of our shows as we play a lot of private events, and to know that our performance was the reason they were all having an amazing night was very gratifying. They came to dance before they went to the bar to get drinks! In my crowd, that's saying something.

My most painful and educational memory would be accidently leaving my microphone backstage at the very start of one of our outdoor shows, hearing the first song begin, forgetting where I left the microphone, and missing our big entrance, which was being videotaped and broadcast live on cable television. Brutal.

Q: Do you have a particular philosophy of life that you embrace?

A: *Breathe. Be here. And accept that nobody knows why.*

CHAPTER 6

Be a Leader: Bring Happiness to the Dance!

BrickHouse Principle Number 6: You must show up, lead, and bring fun every day!

The best leaders are charismatic. They have the ability to change and control the atmosphere of any room they enter. They are operating from their own agenda on their own time. They are clear on their mission and destination. This clarity gives them confidence and personal power. Rather than reacting to others, others seem to react to them. We want you to have that same power – and we want you to use that power to do amazing things.

The BrickHouse Philosophy says, "Bring happiness to the dance."

Intelligent and charismatic leaders also know how to be happy. They are not waiting for someone else to make them happy. They've taken control of that. Among the questions I'll ask in an interview of a prospective employee is, "Do you go to the dance seeking happiness, or do you bring happiness to the dance?" Obviously, the question is metaphorical in nature but the enlightened leaders immediately see where I'm going. They always answer that they're bringing happiness to the dance.

Charismatic leaders do not wait for someone to amuse them, entertain them, love them or save them. They are in charge of themselves. Nor do they wait for someone to hire them, feed them, nurture them, or tuck them in at night. They've got that covered as well.

Charismatic leaders do not wait for someone to give them their big break. They are too busy *creating* their big break. That doesn't mean that they won't take advantage of an opportunity when it is presented. It simply means that they're not waiting around until it comes along.

It's important to make a distinction about charismatic people. Just because certain people have charisma does not automatically mean they are leaders. There are plenty of charismatic people out there who are sociopaths. They will use their charm to abuse or take advantage of you. Those people are not leaders. Leaders are people who are diligently adding value for customers and making a positive contribution to society.

Charismatic leaders are incredibly self-aware. They stay optimistic and motivated in the face of challenge. Their optimism rubs off on everyone around them. They recognize that simply managing their mood can contribute to a positive business outcome. Moods are contagious. As such, charismatic leaders are skilled in the *creation of atmosphere*. They understand that the atmosphere of their business is primarily their responsibility. Thus, they are conscious of the kind of environment they create.

Charismatic leaders have a certain life force that translates to a joy in living. They bring uplifting energy to a room. They show up every day and bring fun. They are not energy vampires sucking the life out of everyone they meet. Instead, they enhance and bring value. I classify charismatic leaders as revenue. They are never an expense.

Because they are emotionally intelligent, charismatic leaders know when to be "on." They know when they have to perform. This has nothing to do with being phony. Think about it. When you are called upon to perform, whether giving a presentation or playing music in a club, aren't you trying to be your best? Aren't you bringing your best self to the table? Of course you are. In that moment, you are trying to deliver an enthusiastic energy to your audience. So why not up the percentage of time that we spend performing and being our best. Instead of bringing that enthusiastic best self to the table ten percent of the time, what if we could bring it all of the time.

You can – or at least you can when you know you have to be "on." You can bring that best self to the forefront in any moment. How? You simply make a decision as to how to feel and act. *You can do this!*

Certain schools of psychology promote the idea that your thoughts control your feelings. In essence, the idea is that your evaluative beliefs and thoughts about an event dictate how you feel about it. Thus, you can change your feelings about any event by modifying your thinking. For example, instead of evaluating a mistake as a catastrophe, you might think of it instead as an inconvenient setback that you will simply correct and learn from. You'll still feel somewhat badly about it but you won't dwell on it or become paralyzed simply because you made a mistake.

I will take this a step further. I believe that we can decide how we want to feel and act in an instant. Don't believe it? Here's a story that I'll bet many of you have lived. Or I'll bet you've seen a situation that played out similarly.

A long time ago, I had a girlfriend. She was mad at me. I know, hard to imagine. But she was just flat-out going off on me. She was yelling, crying and seemingly out of control. I'm sure that she and anyone witnessing this would have said that her feelings were genuine and completely beyond her control in that moment. As the recipient of her wrath, I would have thought so too. That is, until the phone rang.

Now unless the telephone set off some kind of conditioned response worthy of one of Pavlov's dogs, what I witnessed seemed practically miraculous. Immediately the tears stopped. The shrieking subsided. She picked up the phone and in an enthusiastic, cheery voice said, "Hello?" Then in a very composed and positive tone that seemed completely opposite from what was being screeched just seconds before, she said, "Oh, how are you? That's wonderful! I'm just fine, doing great!"

I remember feeling stunned while watching this. I did not understand how someone who seemed so genuinely upset could immediately become so calm and happy. But since then, I've seen this kind of turnaround occur many times. In fact, I've had moments just before going on stage when I was handling some kind of technical problem that I had allowed to upset me. Yet I had to perform just seconds later. The instant I had to perform I switched "on" and became my best performer self. This was a choice and having done it, I know that I can make that choice in any moment. Having seen this ability in others and having done it myself, I now know that we can control our feelings in an instant.

The best leaders know how and when they have to be on. They know when they have to turn the switch and become enthusiastic, energetic, happy performers. They are masters of managing themselves in the moment. There is an old saying, *leave your problems at the stage door*. The most successful leaders and performers can do this every time.

That stage door might be your office. It might be a speaker's podium. It might be a client's front door as you go in to close a sale. It might even be your front door as you come home to your family after a hard day at work. Whatever it is, when it's time to deliver, let go of your problems and commit your full attention to the task at hand. That's what winners do.

The BrickHouse Philosophy says, "Be an ACE!"

Sometimes being a leader can be very stressful. You may want to melt down. You may lose your patience. You may want to yell at people. That's normal and it doesn't make you a bad person. But at those times, it's helpful to remember that your success in leading and managing others depends entirely on how well you manage yourself. The emotionally intelligent leader understands that blame, finger pointing and drama will eventually backfire. Why? Because it's human nature to want to get even. People are like elephants, they never forget. No one wants to be slighted or made to look foolish. If you melt down, there will be a consequence. It might not happen right away, but it will eventually come and you will suffer for your actions.

If you have unlimited time and unlimited money, perhaps you can be a jerk and succeed. You could fire someone every day, manage by intimidation and take all the time you need getting replacements up to speed. And certainly, a case can be made for the fact that sometimes people who fear for their jobs will actually work harder – at least for awhile. But who wants to live like that? I certainly don't and I don't advocate the "manage by fear" strategy. Life is too short to operate in an environment built on fear. Besides, customers and potential employees can smell fear a mile away. They will run from any environment where intimidation is evident.

Interestingly, like certain companies, some bands operate like this. The musicians get fined for mistakes. The band leader usually sports an enormous ego and while talented, the leader makes the entire enterprise a joyless experience for everyone. And customers can sense it.

In addition to being stressful, sometimes being a leader is just not fun. You have to work harder. You have to sacrifice. There will be times when you are deeply disappointed. But great leaders recognize that they must push beyond what an ordinary person would do.

There may be times when, as the leader, you will have to hold everyone's fatigue, fear and frustration in your own giant cup of awareness. It takes an extreme amount of character to do this. It requires being bigger than your own issues and setting the best example you possibly can, while recognizing that you too are only human. How you react to a problem often has a bigger influence on your team's morale and productivity than the problem itself.

Quite simply, you have to be bigger than your problems. You have to hold your head up when everyone else's is hanging. Believe me, there will be times when you want to hang yours more than anyone. After all, you're probably more invested than anyone, emotionally, financially and otherwise. But the truth is, you *are* bigger than all of it.

During these times, you have to react with poise, optimism, reassurance and courage. You have to go back to picturing your destination and making sure everyone remembers what you are doing and why. Help everyone on your team revisit who they are and what they are about. If you can do that, solutions to problems will begin to surface. As a leader, you are there to solve problems and create opportunities for everyone to succeed. Great leaders are all about helping their teams advance. Your ability to help others improve, grow and advance is really your measure as a leader.

There are two worlds; the inside world and the outside world. You control the inside one. You can project the confidence and never-say-die attitude that winners have. When you catch yourself with your head hanging, just remember who you are and what you're about. Remember the destination and remind yourself that no matter how distant it seems, you must advance.

How do you do this, particularly when everything seems to be going against you?

You do it by becoming an ACE! ACE is an acronym that stands for *attention, carriage and emotions*. Remembering that you have control of these three factors can help you to *Always Advance*.

Be an ACE

Control your ATTENTION.

The difference between victory and defeat ultimately comes down to your ability to commit sustained attention to your task. If you can home in on the most important thing that needs doing in the moment, you will give yourself the chance to succeed.

Control your CARRIAGE.

Stand up straight. Sit tall. Walk tall. Radiate magnetic power. Look people in the eye. This will dramatically affect how you feel and how you function. If you want to be proud, strong and unstoppable, stand, walk and talk the way a proud, strong and unstoppable person would. Turn on charisma by clearly remembering your destination and why you are going there. Turn on your energy switch. Use your vitality to push past normal fatigue.

Control your EMOTIONS.

Outside of physically assaulting you, no one has the power to make you feel anything without your consent. Take charge of your mind. We assign meanings to everything that happens. It helps to be objective and simply deal with facts. Do not "attribute" motives to other people when you don't know why they are acting a certain way. They are responsible for their feelings and behaviors. You are responsible for yours. *Choose* the emotion you want to feel. Get big. Leave your problems at the stage door.

"But I'm tired," you say. "And I'm frustrated," you add. Of course you are! You're human and humans get tired and frustrated. But humans also have an amazing capacity to move beyond their fatigue and frustration. This is particularly true when they are resolved to getting a task accomplished. When you are totally absorbed and engaged in an activity, you can stay up for a very long time and expend a tremendous amount of energy. Tap into that by becoming an ACE.

While many books that address leadership speak to methods of leading others, very few address how a leader handles the challenge of working alone. When you are stuck late at the office by yourself, can you keep working? Can you manage yourself in the moment when it's not glamorous and you're tired? Can you commit sustained attention to your task when there is no one watching? When there is no applause? Can you keep going when you know other people are out having a good time?

This is when remembering to be an ACE can help you advance and win. There have been many Friday nights before a Saturday performance when I knew my team was out having a social life. I, on the other hand, was home programming backup systems for the midi sequencing in the unlikely event our technology failed. Or I was preparing and printing the play lists. Or I was even working on a project like this book

It takes consistently applied, dedicated effort to *Always Advance*. Brooke has also taken a true leadership role. Many nights she has worked alone to edit video, answer e-mails or book shows. Other times she has worked all night sewing costumes to have them ready for a show while I slept. She knows what it takes to be successful and has never wavered in her resolve.

You can't be heroic when it's easy. You can only be heroic when it's hard. When others shut down, you can step up. You can move forward and advance. When others are whining about their lot and blaming circumstances for their situation, you can join the winners who have already moved on. The winners are committing single-minded, sustained attention on the task at hand. Strive to be one of them. Strive to be an ACE.

The BrickHouse Philosophy says, "If you're living vicariously, you're not really living."

In order to be a leader, you have to show up for your own life. What does it mean to show up for your own life? It means to bring the same energy, commitment and enthusiasm to every performance, to every job, every day. Your customer deserves that. Your employer deserves that. Your employees deserve it as well. Most importantly, *you* deserve that. You want to be evaluated and remembered as the person who left it all on the playing field, spent but exhilarated.

But in order to leave it all on the playing field, you have to declare yourself a player in the game. You have to believe in your own capabilities. You have to believe that *you are enough*.

In fact, you *are* enough. The same human "stuff" that flows through the people you admire runs through you as well. Whether you want to call it universal intelligence or cosmic energy or just plain blood and guts, you've got what everybody else has. Maybe up until now, you've never believed you had greatness in you. Wrong. You can be as great as you desire to be. But you must make the decision to actually show up!

It's easy to think that life would be good if only it was somebody else's life, or if I could just lose thirty pounds, or if it was just fifteen years ago. But you are right here, right now, standing in the middle of your own existence. And you can work from this point, with what you have, to become who you want to be and get the life that you want. You can make a difference in this world – to yourself and to others. You can contribute mightily. This is your wakeup call.

You don't need permission. There is no need to wait. The clock is ticking. No one is going to beg you to join in. It's your call. But if you are living through other people's achievements, you are living vicariously. If that's okay with you, fine. But if there is a small ember inside of you that is burning to get out and impact the world, honor it. Pay attention to that voice inside you that says *I am more than this*.

Former Navy SEAL and best-selling author Richard Machowicz taught me that there are two ways to approach each day. One approach is to wake up and ask, *what's going to happen to me today?* The other approach is to ask, *what am I going to get done?*

Do you see the difference? The first question is replete with fear. It will take you to a place where you question your own ability. It will take you to a place where you become concerned about what the world and the people in it are going to do to you.

The second question is much more proactive. It leads you to a place where you are acting upon the world. You're not waiting for something to happen to you. You are instead making things happen. It reminds me of a time when I was interviewing an executive in the aerospace business. In talking with him I mentioned that it must be difficult being in a job where there was so much stress. His response took me by surprise. He said, "I don't *have* stress. I *give* stress."

While I don't recommend *giving* stress, I could appreciate the idea behind this approach. This executive was operating from a proactive position. He wasn't the least bit concerned about what the world had in store for him. He was concentrating on what he had in store for the world. Quite simply, he was busy making things happen.

You can either be a watcher or a player. If you declare yourself in and become a player, you can use the time you have left. From wherever you're at, you now know that with the right skill, enough courage and unmitigated resolve, you can advance further than you have ever imagined. Why not try and do something you've always wanted to do. Sure, it's easier to sit back and be entertained – and it's probably more relaxing. But if you've ever felt that there is more to you and to what you could actually accomplish, maybe you should go for it.

Our time on the planet is limited. But the human spirit is not. If you're tired of watching, there is still time to get into the game.

The BrickHouse Philosophy says, "Age is no excuse; in fact, there are no excuses."

The challenges that people face are pretty much the same. Few of us live completely charmed or completely cursed lives. So what is it that finally separates the winners from everyone else?

It boils down to this. Winners have given up excuses. They simply don't accept them. They accept only the results they have pursued.

There are always a million reasons as to why you cannot or should not attempt something. Many of them may be quite compelling. Brooke and I heard all of them when we began The BrickHouse Band.

The reasons for not succeeding were plenty. And in fact, we didn't know if we would succeed when we began. There are no guarantees of success for anyone. But failure is certainly guaranteed if you don't make the attempt. You have to swing the bat if you're going to get a hit. So we simply committed to the attempt. We agreed to *Always Advance* towards our destination. Sometimes it meant taking a step back in order to go forward. But we kept grinding away. During the journey, we came up with a concept we'd like to share.

Mid-life Mastery

A wise person once said that it's never too late to be what you might have been. Brooke and I have certainly found that to be true. Experience combined with committed energy can be a formidable package. As such, we'd like to introduce you to the concept of Mid-life Mastery.

What is Mid-life Mastery? It is the idea that you can truly live the life that you want through your middle years and beyond. But you don't have to wait until you are in your 40's or 50's to learn the lessons. You can pursue your interests, work towards greater health and maintain a terrific appearance beginning at any age.

To be a mid-life master does not mean that you have every answer or that you've solved every problem. It simply means that you continue to leverage your experience while keeping yourself in the best physical and mental condition of which you are capable.

No matter what age you are, now is the time to be passionate about who you are and what you want to do. Why? Because now is the only time you have!

If you didn't have the perceived limitation of age, what would you accomplish? Age is really a side issue. It's other people's stuff and it doesn't have to be yours. If you are living your passion, doing what you want to do, and most importantly, *delivering the product*, age won't matter. The bottom line is always – can you deliver? If you can, you can set an example for what is possible at any age!

Here are the tenets of Mid-life Mastery.

1. *Resist all labels that do not serve you.*

   Labels distance people from one another. They are designed to separate people and put them into a box. Young, old, smart, stupid, black, white, fast or slow, these are all attempts to stereotype and categorize people. Don't accept a label someone else gives you that doesn't serve your best interests.

2. *Leverage your years of experience.*

   Use what you've learned to your advantage. If you haven't learned the lessons of mid-life, you probably deserve to suffer! Mature, experienced people make their own rules. These rules are judged by one criterion; do they work? Think independently. Listen to your gut. When the World Trade Center collapsed on September 11th, 2001, hundreds of workers were trapped in the towers. Security personnel told them to stay put and wait for help. The ones who survived didn't wait. They headed down the stairs through the smoke-filled stairwells. They didn't blindly follow instructions and as a result, they lived.

3. *Vow to work more on yourself and less on other people.*

   There is a strong tendency to want to share our experiences with others. But be careful not to tell people what they *should* be doing. Instead, continue to work on yourself and set an example that others might want to follow. Don't *tell* people how awesome you are; *show* people how awesome you are. They'll figure it out.

4. *Seek out examples of those who are flourishing in mid-life.*

   There are numerous examples of people achieving remarkable things in mid-life and well beyond. One of my favorites is actor and martial artist Chuck Norris. Chuck is currently 68 years old. His physical and mental condition is astounding. His work ethic and exercise habits are worth examining to see if you might want to emulate them. Find examples of people who are succeeding through their middle years and beyond. Then resolve to become one of them.

5. *Embrace discomfort and continue to advance.*

Be willing to stretch and get out of your comfort zone. Growth involves change and change is sometimes uncomfortable. It won't always feel good and you won't always look good. But the gains and the growth are worth it.

6. *Commit to your health.*

   This is a no-brainer. Your body is less forgiving as you get older. There is less of a margin for error. Yes, it's not fair. So what, no one cares. You must practice good health habits in order to be the best you can be. Commit to exercise, proper nutrition and rest. We must eliminate the excuses of "I'm too tired" and "I'm too out of shape." Those are conditions that can be overcome.

7. *Recognize your power.*

   Who are you not to be a hero? Ultimately, you simply say, *I am*. Then you get up and prove it. Time will catch up to you, but only if you are standing still. There is power in movement. If you're not finished, keep going. You must move in order to advance.

So what is next for you? What is it that you want to do? What do you want to create?

I believe that there is a heroic journey within each of us. Using the six principles outlined in this book, you can move forward towards the destination of your choosing.

1. Decide where you are going and why.
2. Research how you need to get there; then do it *your* way.

3. Make full use of your skills, your courage and your resolve.
4. Suspend your ego and employ emotional intelligence to gain a competitive advantage.
5. Leverage everything that happens to you.
6. Show up, lead and bring fun every day!

Your destination awaits you. Your journey begins right now. The question isn't whether you *can* do something great...the question is whether you *will*.

When you're tired, when you're frustrated, when everyone says you're too old or too inexperienced; when you feel that everything is going against you, can you find it within yourself - in that moment - to advance towards your destination?

I'm betting you can.

Key Points from Chapter Six

- Charismatic leaders are in charge of themselves. They bring fun and happiness to the dance.
- Know when it's time to perform and be "on." Leave your problems at the stage door and pay attention to the task at hand.
- As a leader, you must be bigger than your problems. Remember who you are and why you're doing what you're doing.
- ACE is an acronym that stands for *attention, carriage and emotions*. Remembering that you have control of these three factors can help you to *Always Advance*.

- You don't have to wait for permission to do what you want to do. Be proactive and commit your attention to what you're going to accomplish.
- Age is no excuse for not going after what you want. You can utilize the tenets of Mid-life Mastery at any age to advance.
- The question isn't whether you *can* do something great...the question is whether you *will*.

BROOKE WITT – Vocals, Dance and Co-founder of Brick-House

Courtesy of Lumina Photography

"Wow, my C.P.A. doesn't look like that!"

Those were the first words I (Lee) ever uttered upon seeing my beautiful wife, Brooke. She was singing karaoke one New Year's Eve while we were both out on dates with different people. Having just been told by friends that she was a Certified Public Accountant, I was somewhat taken aback. They also told me that she was a mother of three and a karaoke host at a local restaurant. Later I learned that she had an extensive theater and dance background with a degree in bacteriology to boot. To say the least, I was intrigued.

Several years, a marriage and one band later we have managed to build the enterprise called The BrickHouse Band. It is mostly due to her diligence, intelligence and remarkable staying power that we have succeeded. And it was her vision of a fully choreographed stage show that has helped us differentiate ourselves from competitors.

Apart from her formidable performance abilities, Brooke has shown the leadership qualities necessary to build a team of solid, quality people. Much of the band's success has been due to her engaging personality and her ability to win people's trust. Behind the scenes, she has handled 90% of the customer and agent contacts. From costuming to sound equipment to choreography, Brooke has built the foundations upon which this band was built.

She has inspired countless numbers of people, showing them that you can achieve great things in mid-life if you work hard and follow solid success principles. A full time C.P.A., wife, mother, singer, dancer, and band leader, she still makes time to work out and eat healthy. The results speak for themselves. In fact, if you were to follow her around for a week, your DNA might just break down. But guaranteed, you'd have a great time!

Our Q & A with Brooke gives you some insights into

what's made her such a success.

Q: What unique quality or qualities do you believe have made you successful both in life and in the band?

A: *The ability to commit my full attention to a task. Watching me during the day, I seem kind of frenetic, but over time, what needs to get done gets done. This was true of a college degree, getting in shape, passing the CPA exam, and developing a choreographed, costumed band with Lee. And oh, a sense of humor helps!*

I also value the power of resolve. When I go for something, I cut off all possibility of failure. In addition, when I'm up against a problem, I try and think "outside-the-box." Every business has unique problems that require unique solutions. I learned as a small business advisor and small business owner that you sometimes need to back up and look at the not-so-obvious.

I also believe in the power of "constructive vanity." For me, this is even more potent than will power. I like looking good. I can't say I'm a health nut, but fortunately the behaviors that lead to improved appearance also tend to be healthy lifestyle choices.

Q: What have you learned from your life experience that you've brought to the band?

A: *Each day begins the night before. The tone of your day, especially if it's a day with a big event, will be set by what you do the night before. If you prepare, you will not be as stressed. You also need to get enough sleep as part of your preparation. Seven or eight hours of sleep will lead to the best days of all.*

Also, I've learned that if you keep doing something, you are more apt to get good at it. Practice really can make perfect. Finally, I've learned that "caffeine is good." Seriously. In college biochemistry we learned that caffeine helps the brain retrieve information (including lyrics, I assume) more easily. Note - too much caffeine is not good. I took a No-Doz and downed two Dr. Peppers one morning before a final exam in chemistry. The resulting jumble of thought processes, while quite fast, didn't help me a bit. So please include the disclaimer.

Q: What have you learned from your band / music experience that you've taken back into your life?

A: *Making a fool of yourself in public can be okay and even endearing to other people, if you have a sense of humor about it. We've all been there. It's a part of the common human experience. On the other hand, the "fake it 'til you make it" theory works, too. I used to be much more traumatized on stage when I would occasionally blow a lyric. In reality, people usually don't even notice. As one of my favorite karaoke hosts says to his singers, "Now get up there and act like you know what you're doing!"*

Something else that's very important is that you're not automatically old when you turn 50. I can do more dance moves than ever before; I can sing more skillfully than when I was younger; I'm in about the best shape I've ever been in - my weight is lower and my muscles more defined than during my senior year of high school. I'm mostly free, for the first time, of my crippling stage fright. However, let's be candid here. It must be remembered that hair dye is critical to looking youthful after 50. A good plastic surgeon, particularly if you've had children, is to be valued as well.

Q: What do you value most about the other members of the band? What have you learned from them?

A: I value that they are so willing to try ideas, musically and theatrically, and sometimes even play music they really dislike. While realizing that "Hollaback Girl" doesn't make much use of the guys' musical abilities, they were still willing to do it for the audience. Craig, our rocker guitarist has been willing to play 40's standards; our very hip "city girl," Kristi has willingly learned harmony to Nikki's new country song. The musicians respect each other, but also cut each other some slack when we make mistakes. Okay sometimes there's a jab, but it's always in fun. The sense of humor never stops rolling and it can be the perfect response to almost every situation (thank you Greg and Lee).

Something else I've learned is that some people have more musical skill than I will ever come close to achieving. However, some of us also have strengths in other areas that give value to the overall show. I've watched the girls, neither of whom had dance training, progress amazingly in dance skills through sheer hard work. I've also learned about true stamina as I've watched each of the others go onstage in major pain, sometimes pre-surgery or post-surgery, without any complaint.

Q: What is your favorite band memory to this point? Any particularly humorous moment? Painful or embarrassing moment? Educational moment?

A: There have been too many favorite moments to mention, but all revolve around the audience reaching a certain "flash point." It's a moment where joyful energy surges up from the dance floor and washes over the stage. We've had particular fun at the Tulalip Casino in Marysville, Washington in addition to the many conventions we've played. It's also been gratifying that both of my daughters have appeared on stage with me, Brittany as part of the band before she returned to college, and Kristine as a dancer. I have loved having them onstage with me

Perhaps the funniest moment was when my daughter Brittany stepped in front of a man who wanted to get too friendly with me at a dance club. This gentleman reached up onto the stage, grabbed my hand between songs and started kissing it. He then moved up my arm. My daughter Brittany stepped over beside me and said loudly and not too gently into her microphone, "Um, THAT'S MY MOM, and THAT'S HER HUSBAND!" jabbing a finger back to Lee on the keyboards. The packed house exploded into uproarious laughter and the college boys howled as they slapped each other on the back and pointed to the stage. The man smiled and backed away; my little tiger cub simmered down, and the fun continued at an even higher level.

Embarrassing moments? There have been a few. The good thing is, I've had so many that I think the embarrassment part of my brain has burned out.

Q: Do you have a particular philosophy of life that you embrace?

A: *You get out of it what you put into it. This is true of everything from math classes to sports to attending a party. It's true of raising children and working at your job. It's definitely true of entertaining. When I get bored or frustrated, I put more into it. I remember to value the customer. The difference in the resulting experience is amazing. Also, I've learned that everybody just wants to be respected. When you show respect, people are more likely to want to like you, and life is easier.*

Conclusion

We stood inside the Seattle area's largest casino. We had been married for five years. A popular local cover band was performing on their gigantic stage. The dance floor was filled with hundreds of joyous people. The energy in the room was electric. I looked up at the giant-sized movie screen projecting the band's image to those in the back.

It was us.

APPENDIX I
The BrickHouse Vision and Mission Package

VISION

The BrickHouse Band is the preferred provider of music and entertainment for corporate events, fundraisers, private parties, casinos, and wedding receptions.

MISSION

To provide sensational value by bringing high-energy, interactive, quality entertainment and outrageous fun to all customers.

OUR CUSTOMERS

Definition of Customers: Those who pay for our services.

Secondary Customers: Those who are touched by

our product in some way. All deserve our respect and attention.

WE CREATE FOR OUR CUSTOMERS:

- A Festive Atmosphere
- Unforgettable Memories
- A Visual Production They Can Enjoy
- Compelling Dance Music
- Warmth and Interaction – A Personal Touch

WHY HIRE BRICKHOUSE?

We DIFFERENTIATE ourselves from the hundreds of other bands you could hire. We bring:

- Outstanding Musicianship
- Unparalleled Vocal Talent
- A Highly Choreographed Show with professional sound and lighting
- Customer Service that Exceeds Expectations

OUR TEAM

The best overall result occurs when we put the good of the whole group ahead of individual recognition. We will always WIN if:

- You show up with your best
- You suspend your ego for the good of the enterprise
- You place your attention on the customer
- You practice emotional intelligence

OUR CODE OF CONDUCT

- We hold ourselves to a higher standard
- We conduct and carry ourselves with class
- We are well-dressed, well-mannered and professional
- With occasional exceptions (e.g., private parties at the end of the evening) we do not use alcohol during performances
- We *BRING IT* every night!

For reference, I (Lee) have included my own personal Vision, Mission and Purpose statements below.

Vision: Have the greatest positive impact while manifesting my inner nature.

Mission and Goal: To expand, encourage and SERVE as a model of health, love, humor, abundance, gratitude and intelligence – and to be a model of possibility for what can be achieved in mid-life.

Purpose: I am inspiring and educating people on how to reach the upper limits of their genetic potential, physically, intellectually and emotionally, so that they can reach the goals they set for themselves, living happier and more productive lives. I give people strategies and tools to help them succeed, because in order to contribute more, they must become more.

APPENDIX II
The *Always Advance* Performance Methodology BrickHouse Principles and Philosophical Maxims

BrickHouse Principle Number 1: You must understand where you're going and why.

The BrickHouse Philosophy says, "Compete until you win."
The BrickHouse Philosophy says, "Always Advance."
The BrickHouse Philosophy says, "If you're not successful in your life, you won't be successful in our band."
The BrickHouse Philosophy says, "Serve the customer and you can stay in the phone book."

BrickHouse Principle Number 2: You must research the market; then do it YOUR way.

The BrickHouse Philosophy says, "If you fail to prepare, prepare to fail."

The BrickHouse Philosophy says, "Know who your REAL customer is."

The BrickHouse Philosophy says, "Your travel plan should include D-S-M-F: Destination-Situation-Map-Fuel."

The BrickHouse Philosophy says, "Don't model their product; make them want to model yours."

BrickHouse Principle Number 3: You must be competent, courageous and resolute.

The BrickHouse Philosophy says, "Cultivate the skill, the chill and the will."

The BrickHouse Philosophy says, "A baseline of competence is necessary, but winning is rarely about talent."

The BrickHouse Philosophy says, "Defeat the fear of death, and welcome the death of fear."

The BrickHouse Philosophy says, "Be unreasonable, unrelenting, and unstoppable."

BrickHouse Principle Number 4: You must suspend your ego for the good of the enterprise.

The BrickHouse Philosophy says, "Without emotional intelligence, your skills, your talent and your I.Q. will not matter."

The BrickHouse Philosophy says, "To find the groove, you've got to get out of your own way."

The BrickHouse Philosophy says, "If you don't care who gets the credit, your team can reach any destination."
The BrickHouse Philosophy says, "A generous and abundant spirit attracts the best of everything."

BrickHouse Principle Number 5: You must leverage everything that happens to you.

The BrickHouse Philosophy says, "In our world, nothing ever goes wrong."
The BrickHouse Philosophy says, "First, you must get their attention."
The BrickHouse Philosophy says, "Leverage Time."
The BrickHouse Philosophy says, "Leverage Energy."

BrickHouse Principle Number 6: You must show up, lead, and bring fun every day!

The BrickHouse Philosophy says, "Bring happiness to the dance."
The BrickHouse Philosophy says, "Be an ACE!"
The BrickHouse Philosophy says, "If you're living vicariously, you're not really living."
The BrickHouse Philosophy says, "Age is no excuse; in fact, there are no excuses."

APPENDIX III
Method for Practicing Mindfulness Meditation

One of America's foremost authorities on mindfulness is Jon Kabat-Zinn. He defines mindfulness meditation as *the practice of paying attention to the unfolding of the present moment - in all its fullness*. The phrase "in all its fullness" is important because when you see something fully, possibilities for new behaviors can sometimes open up.

Our mindfulness practice is perhaps not as rigorous as other disciplines. This is because we want you to be comfortable initially and stay with your practice. It's easy to get discouraged initially because *just sitting* seems so counter to our everyday lives. Once you have gained some momentum and consistency with your practice, you might become interested in exploring other forms of meditation. For example, certain practices in the Zen traditions, as well as Transcendental Meditation, take a more structured approach that rely on certain postures as you meditate. They can be a bit more demanding, but the rewards have been well documented.

The BrickHouse practice is simply designed to help you become more aware. Once you realize that you can hold your thoughts, your impulses, fears and desires in the giant container of your mind, you can begin to recognize them for what they are. You can recognize a thought and sit with it. Instead of immediately judging it and acting on it, you can recognize that you're having an impulse to do something. Whether you follow through or not is up to you – but you give yourself options and you are acting with awareness. You're not just mindlessly reacting to whatever pops into your head. You actually *recognize* that it is popping into your head and you have the choice as to what you want to do with it.

This recognition gives you insight into the person you are. It gives you insight into how you behave and why. It gives you the option to change and grow if you so desire.

Your mindfulness meditation practice does not have to be complicated. If you like routine, it might help if you can find a place that you go to each day. But part of the beauty of a meditation practice is that you can do it anywhere. Even if you are on the road for your business you can meditate in a hotel, in a car, or a city park. It does not require anything other than your presence.

Many people have the idea that meditation is an escape from reality. In fact, the exact opposite is true. It's about tuning in to reality and paying attention to what's happening in the precise moment you're in.

You don't need to sit in the lotus position or put your

ankles behind your head. Just find a comfortable position either sitting or lying down. It might be more accurate to call this a "relaxation" practice. There are a number of very valuable meditation practices that require certain postures. But they are more about helping you get in touch with how your mind responds to your body's discomfort. For our purposes, we are interested in helping you simply become present to the now. If you can relax and lower your blood pressure during this time, that's even better.

I use a chair. If you're seated, try and keep your posture strong while remaining relaxed. It's good if your head, neck and trunk can be aligned. If you're seated, you may place your hands on your thighs or position them in a manner that is comfortable. If lying down, assume what is called the relaxed body position. Keep your legs straight and slightly apart. Your arms should be at your sides and not touching the body. Your palms can be up or down depending upon what is most comfortable for you. The perfect posture is the one that is comfortable for you.

Loosen up any clothing that might be too tight, particularly around the waist. We don't want anything to impede our ability to breathe deeply.

Take slow and deep breaths in through the nose. Breathing in through the nose helps to filter out impurities and toxins. It also warms the air. If you have sinus problems that prevent you from nose breathing, obviously, you'll need to breathe through your mouth. But to the extent possible, breathe through your nose.

Breathe from the diaphragm. This will enable more air to fill the lungs, thus increasing your lung capacity. You should feel your abdomen rising with inhalation, and falling with exhalation. Your chest should not move a great deal.

In some meditation practices, eyes remain open. I prefer to close mine. Again, I'm all about relaxation in this instance. As you inhale and exhale, you can just think to yourself, "In" and "Out." It sounds easy but you'll find your thoughts beginning to wander after a few moments. Don't be angry or upset if this happens. However, if you find yourself getting angry, don't judge yourself harshly for it, simply notice it. Simply notice how interesting it is when you feel an emotion. When you catch your thoughts wandering, simply go back to thinking "In" and "Out."

After a while, you may choose to just sit, breathe and relax. Just concentrate on what is happening in this present moment. What are the sounds? What are the smells? What are the physical sensations occurring right now? Just sit with those – and notice.

If you find your thoughts wandering into what happened yesterday or what might happen later, just smile and bring yourself back to your breath. This one breath that you're taking right now is all that matters...until the next one.

When you are finished, slowly reenter the world. Think about who you are and where you are. Now you can begin to think about what you need to do. Then, carry a centered mind at peace into your world.

Again, your local library, bookstores and the internet have a wealth of information on meditation that you can benefit from. For now, just stop for a moment. Listen to your breath, watch your thoughts, and recognize that you are not tuning out, you're actually tuning in.

APPENDIX IV
Sample Checklist for Band Show

In chapter two, we suggested that checklists can be helpful in preparation. Here is a sample checklist of equipment that we pack for a show when we are providing the sound equipment and lighting. You can use a similar checklist for any preparations that you are consistently called upon to perform.

EQUIPMENT

- Rack for Wireless headsets/microphones
- Lee's Rack for Computer and Power Conditioner
- Smart cards with backup sequences
- Ipod and cables for 3rd backup system
- Monitors for side-fill stage sound
- Monitors for guitarists (if necessary)
- Speaker cable bag with all required cables
- Microphone cable bag
- Extension cord crate with power strips

- Stage Ninja Power Strips (2)
- Light Trees
- Light Bars
- T4 Light Chaser
- Extension cords for lights
- Wireless microphones and in-ear monitors
- Batteries
- Wired Microphones
- Mackie Main Sound Board
- Table for sound board (if necessary)
- Small Mackie Board if using stage monitors
- Hand truck
- JBL Speakers for mids and highs
- JBL Subs for lows
- Poles for speakers
- Back-up Amp
- Rack and roller
- Rack #2
- CD player and CDs for in-between sets
- Snake (large or small)
- Music stands and lights
- Flashlights
- 2 or 3 Korg Triton Keyboards (3rd is backup)
- Korg Stand and Legs
- Boom for the Korg Stand
- Keyboard Foot Pedal
- Percussion Stand with instruments
- Drummer click-track bag with headphones and cords

- Band brochures, Business cards
- Tickets for Give-away (if we are giving away a prize, for example a CD Player)
- Ticket vase to hold tickets
- Feather boas (for audience)
- Tambourines (for audience)
- Light-up maracas (for audience)
- Printed Set Lists
- Lyrics (if necessary)

CLOTHES, MAKE-UP AND MISCELLANEOUS ITEMS

- Skirts and tops
- Tux vests and ties (if necessary)
- Sequin shirts (if necessary)
- Dance Shoes
- Hats
- Earrings
- Bracelets
- Nylons
- Eyelashes
- Eyeliner
- Lip liner
- Lipstick
- Hairspray
- Eye shadow
- Contact Lenses and solution
- Reading Glasses
- Bobby pins
- Hair clips

- Toothbrush and toothpaste
- Protein Bars
- Throat Spray
- Aspirin
- Decongestant
- $ for Sound Engineer

APPENDIX V
Bibliography and Suggested Reading

Unleash the Warrior Within by Richard J. Machowicz

No Excuse Leadership by Brace Barber

Slow Down by David Essel

Man's Search for Meaning by Victor Frankl

Emotional Intelligence by Daniel Goleman

Working With Emotional Intelligence by Daniel Goleman

Executive E.Q. by Robert Cooper

Your Erroneous Zones by Wayne Dyer

Pulling Your Own Strings by Wayne Dyer

Return to Love by Marianne Williamson

Full Catastrophe Living by Jon Kabat-Zinn

Wherever You Go, There You Are by Jon Kabat-Zinn

Operation Excellence by Mark Bender

Lead or Get Off the Pot by Pat Croce

Flow by Mihaly Csikszentmihalyi

You Are the Message by Roger Ailes

Become Unstoppable by Lee Witt

Getting What You Want by Robert J. Ringer

Silent Power by Stuart Wilde

Awaken the Giant Within by Anthony Robbins

You Play to Win the Game by Herman Edwards

Executive Charisma by D.A. Benton

Be, Know, Do by Frances Hesselbein, General Eric K. Shinseki, and R. Cavanagh

Will by G. Gordon Liddy

Zen in the Martial Arts by Joe Hyams

City Dharma by Arthur Jeon

Compassionate Samurai by Brian Klemmer

The Power of Now by Eckhart Tolle

Take Control by Michael Janke

Shut Up, Stop Whining, and Get a Life by Larry Winget

The Secret of Inner Strength by Chuck Norris with Joe Hyams

The Secret Power Within by Chuck Norris

Acknowledgements

There are so many people that have helped me along this path. My most gracious thanks to:

Brooke Witt, Dale Drenner, Craig Coleman, Greg Backstrom, Nikki Stewart and Kristi Evans. While the sum is greater than the parts, the parts are pretty terrific too!

Richard, Mandy, and Josie Machowicz for their inspirational teachings and example.

Brace Barber for truly understanding leadership and his commitment to all things good.

David Essel for guidance, love and always being there.

All BrickHouse alumni and in particular, our on-call, ready musicians, Lawrence Hightower and Tom Lash. You guys are studs.

David Harris for his professionalism, musical knowledge, great advice and friendship.

Mike Allen for the fantastic studio and sound work from the beginning. You're an honored BrickHouse member.

Kirk Riley for always making us sound our best under any circumstance. You always make it work.

Josh Dunham for your hard work and sound expertise. Good things are ahead for you, young man.

Bob and Shelley Tomberg for helping us learn how this band thing works. Go Shelley and the Curves!

Ben Thorsteinson for his insights into the world of cover bands. His belief in us from the beginning truly helped us advance.

Terry Quick at ENTCO Inc. for opening doors and giving us some opportunities to seize.

Ceasar Cabral at Studio C for his outstanding talent in website development and design.

Glen Sayes and his team at Lumina for outstanding photography, service and advice.

Dr. Floyd Hoelting for his help, friendship and guidance when I was young, and once again now that I'm older.

James Webb for demonstrating how much you can get done in one lifetime.

Pat Croce for continuous positive inspiration.

The men of Illinois State University, Bob Jehli, Mike Zeman, Dave Kozlowski and the late Dan Youssi. Gladly would he learn and gladly teach.

My children; Landeau, Kristine and Brittany and my grandchildren, Keisha and Kaleb. I love you all beyond measure.

My sister Karen Jepsen and her children, Andrew and Kira. You guys rock!

My mother-in-law, Corinne Balser and father-in-law, Dick Balser – your love and support are truly appreciated.

My other wonderful in-laws for their constant love and support - Sue Shanahan and her late husband Larry, along with their children, Kerri, Kim and Rick; Merle and Cindy Meyers along with their children, Dustin and Morgan, and Dayna Loechelt, along with her children Jessica, Jill and Jeremy.

Chuck Clark, Ann Brittain, Dennis Treece, Kevin Jones, and Steve and Lucinda Olds for intelligence, friendship, talent and fine examples of humanity at its best. The world can never have enough good people.

Hire BrickHouse for the Day!

Always Advance: Building Better Business by Building Better People

Your company deserves the best. Hire BrickHouse and you'll not only get the west coast's best corporate party band for your evening celebration, you'll also get a day of activity and training that you'll never forget. Personal growth was never this entertaining and fun!

Choose one of two morning activities:

- ***Cardio and resistance training class** (beginners and advanced)*
- ***Dance class** (Learn rumba, samba, swing and more!)*

Choose one of four afternoon 2-hour seminars:

- ***The Always Advance Performance Methodology***

  Learn the principles that enabled The BrickHouse Band to overcome all obstacles and reach their business and artistic goals.
- ***Taking Emotional Intelligence to the Next Level: Your Personal and Professional Competitive Advantage***

  Learn what separates the rock stars of business from the also- rans. Your management team and star performers will love this seminar!
- ***Mid-Life Mastery***

Age is no excuse. Learn how to leverage your experience to achieve your goals at any age!

- ***So You Want to Be A Rock Star: Music as a Way of Life***

  Learn how to break into the music business. In addition, we'll demonstrate how applying a professional approach and systematic methodology to your craft can propel you forward in any occupation.

In the evening, it's time to celebrate!

- ***The BrickHouse Music and Party Experience!***

  The BrickHouse Band will treat you to a night of entertainment that you'll always remember. Bring your dancin' shoes or just sit back and enjoy a great show. The BrickHouse Band will create the perfect ending to the perfect day!

Visit www.brickhouseleadership.com for more details.

Visit www.brickhouseband.com
to learn more about the band.

About The Author

Businessman, author, musician and athlete, Lee Witt has over twenty years of experience in communications and project management in the aerospace business. Now CEO of BrickHouse Leadership Solutions, Inc., he and his team train corporations, organizations and schools in the principles of high performance, emotional intelligence, business growth and health. In 2008 Lee authored *Become Unstoppable: Take a Different Stance in Life to Stand Up, Stand Out and Deliver Your Best* from Outskirts Press. The book outlines the eight key components for developing an unstoppable human. Lee was also a featured contributor to *The Worst Case Business Scenario Survival Guide* released from Wiley Publishing in September of 2009.

When not writing, consulting or performing with the band, Lee is a popular keynote speaker at businesses, organizational meetings and community events. He occasionally performs solo as a nightclub pianist and singer – and serves as master of ceremonies for many northwest functions.

Lee holds a Bachelor's Degree in Political Science from Illinois State University.